Aha Moments

When God Reveals a Hidden Meaning

LINDA LAFOON

InspiringVoices

Copyright © 2014 Linda Lafoon.

All rights reserved. No part of this book may be used or reproduced by any means, graphic, electronic, or mechanical, including photocopying, recording, taping or by any information storage retrieval system without the written permission of the publisher except in the case of brief quotations embodied in critical articles and reviews.

Inspiring Voices books may be ordered through booksellers or by contacting:

Inspiring Voices
1663 Liberty Drive
Bloomington, IN 47403
www.inspiringvoices.com
1 (866) 697-5313

Because of the dynamic nature of the Internet, any web addresses or links contained in this book may have changed since publication and may no longer be valid. The views expressed in this work are solely those of the author and do not necessarily reflect the views of the publisher, and the publisher hereby disclaims any responsibility for them.

Any people depicted in stock imagery provided by Thinkstock are models, and such images are being used for illustrative purposes only. Certain stock imagery © Thinkstock.

ISBN: 978-1-4624-1002-6 (sc)
ISBN: 978-1-4624-1003-3 (e)

Library of Congress Control Number: 2014910947

Printed in the United States of America.

Inspiring Voices rev. date: 10/14/2014

Contents

Foreword vii
Introduction ix

Trapped 1
Then the Children Prayed 5
Abraham 9
Christmas 16
Feet and Fragrance 22
No Room 27
Pedicure 31
Cold, Gray Rain 34
Timeout 39
Baaaa 42
Tokens of Love 43
Prognosis: Miracle 46
Winning a Battle 54
The Next Chapter in Our Life Book 56
Saying Good-bye 62
Near Miss 64
Diamonds in Brown Paper 67
I'm Late 71
We Need Rain 74

For Older Women Only 76
Christmas Cards 78
Message from a Thesaurus 82
Rivletts 84
Brown and Gray 87
The Sapling 89
It Is Finished 92
Surprise! 94
Porpoise Syndrome 96
Poinsettias 98
Now I Lay Me Down to Sleep 102
And the Rest of the Story 107

Epilogue 111

Foreword

Like you, I've heard it all. God speaks through the Bible, but I wanted something more direct and personal. I wanted, like Moses, to hear God. And then one day, God opened my ears (and my eyes), and I got what He was saying. That was my aha moment—the moment when I finally got it. I inhaled deeply, and then as I exhaled, I quietly whispered-out, "Aha." I was able to hear God in a unique and wonderful way. And once I'd found the key, more and more doors opened to additional aha moments.

In the pages that follow, I'd like to share a few of those moments with you. Some of these pages contain true stories, and some are fictional. (You'll quickly see which ones.) But I hope you'll find aha moments, and I hope you'll have your own personal talk-time with the Creator of the Universe.

Introduction

I've been laughed at and laughed with. I've cried, and I've caused others to cry. I'm too conservative, too liberal; I'm a know-it-all and a know-nothing-at-all. Discouraged? Disconnected? Delighted? Yep, I've been there. Betrayed and befriended—me again. If you fit into any of those categories, this may be just what you need to let you know that you're not alone.

I know the path you're walking. Somewhere in this book, I think you'll find—well, *you*. You'll find a place where you connect, where you belong. If you feel the night is so dark you can touch it, know that I've been in that darkness. The dark pressed in so hard, I didn't think I could manage the next breath. If you feel no one has a life chapter similar to yours, you may find one close to it here. Too often, those of us who call ourselves Christians don't share the tough times. When anyone asks us, "How are you doing?" we put on that Christian smile and say, "Fine." (You know the word we all use.) Often, though, we are anything but fine. We are hurting, miserable, and alone. And that is when God whispers His answers to our hearts. Sometimes those whispers are deafening.

Bear with me a minute here. Say to a friend, "I really like you, but ..." The friend will never hear the *I really like you,* only the words after *but*. Or hear from the lips of someone who is an integral part of your life, "I love you, but...," you never fully grasp the *I love you part;* you wait for the crushing statement that follows. You'll find I often veer off on rabbit paths like that. But (oh, there's that word) when I veer off, I hope it is for a solid reason. For those who look for that something that is missing, I hope you'll find it in this book. It was written by someone who may have walked the life-path you're on. I've got the blisters, scars, and calluses to prove it. You can count on me to understand where you are. As you read the next pages, I hope you'll laugh some, cry some, and realize that there is someone who understands. I hope you'll see that God whispers time and again in ways He hopes we'll comprehend what He wants us to learn and gain from that experience.

Warning: this book may contain statements with which you do not agree. That's okay. The Constitution that gives me the freedom of speech gives you the right to disagree. I don't mind honest challenges; it shows that thought has been given to the subject. This is a good thing. Disagreement means a nerve has been struck. Some of the best learning moments I have experienced were because I disagreed with something and began a full onslaught of investigation to prove my point. Sometimes I was even right. But right or wrong, I learned a lot. Stubborn people like me dig in for the fight; when we butt heads with others enough times, our necks get stronger. So if you disagree, prove me wrong—build those neck muscles. It's cheaper than going to the gym (and you don't have to shower afterward). Some passages in this book are humorous. Others have a point to make. Read them or skip them. It's your book, and it is up to you.

Now for a disclaimer—I am not given to being politically correct. I simply am unable to keep up with what is correct for the current culture. I offer my apology to anyone I may offend. In being honest and shooting straight from the holster, my aim may not be one that is without abrasion, but I will be as open as I can be. I write from real-life experiences. In cases where I think someone may be harmed and to avoid lawsuits, I have changed the names, places, and some of the supporting information to protect the innocent and the guilty—and sometimes to protect myself. The basic facts are true, but the fluff around them has been altered.

All of us move along with everyday events when life happens. It is in the midst of daily routines, hectic schedules, bumper-to-bumper traffic, and full calendars that the essence of life is revealed. Because we often do not tune-out the noise of life, God whispers. Those tender, whispered words that relay His love and lessons come roaring into our hearts and lives. I hope the crescendo of that whisper will wash over you in a thunderous exhilaration of wonder. Here's praying you'll have aha moments.

Trapped

My elementary-school-aged grandson has a keen eye for animals, especially lizards, frogs, and anything that may show up on Animal Planet. He calls me Bo, or more often, "Hey, Bo." He and I were enjoying a Bo day, and his parents were enjoying a date night. I had purchased a pizza that he and I would eat for dinner. As we sat down in the kitchen to eat, he spotted a hummingbird in my Florida room, which is adjacent to the kitchen. The tiny bird kept fluttering around the ceiling, desperately wanting to be free. We opened both side doors and shut the blinds so that the bird would be able to see the openings, go to one of the doors, and wing its way to freedom. We sat and watched as we ate until the last crumb of our pizza had been consumed. The bird continued to try desperately to find an opening in the ceiling; she did not go to the doorways, as we had hoped. To help guide her, I picked up a broom and used it to direct the bird to the door, just trying to shepherd her to the right path. Darting and gliding, the tiny creature escaped the roundup each time, skillfully maneuvering around the broom and going back to roost on the chain that attached a light to the ceiling.

How small she was—how delicate and fragile. Not wanting to wear out the little bird or scare her to death, we left her alone. Our thought was that as night came, the doorway openings would become more prominent, and the bird would see her way to escape. At midnight, roosting safe and comfortably but not free, the little bird still sat on the chain. Our two home protectors, Tux and Trei, dogs adopted from a local rescue group and of unknown parentage, walked beneath the throne of the tiny hummingbird queen. She eyed them carefully, tilting her head ever so royally. A human passing by caused her only to tilt her head again and look, but she did not fly. It was too dark, and there were too many predators and too much to fear in the night. Dawn would change that, I reasoned.

At 5:30 a.m., 6:00, and 6:30, the doors were still open. The sun had risen, and the day was cloudy but bright. Still, the tiny hummingbird queen sat frozen in fear—frozen to the chain that had become her sense of safety. I couldn't help but think she was chained by her own unwillingness to choose freedom, let me help, and allow guidance to the outside and freedom. Rain was predicted, and I had to go to work. I couldn't leave the doors open. Silent words formed as I tried to relay concern for her. "Fragile, beautiful creation, you will have to leave this area, or you will die. There will be no food for you. You will be safe but not free. Please, please go now."

Again, I used the broom to gently, carefully, and cautiously direct her to the opening. The bird chirped—such a delicate sound from a tiny one. But it was a sound of fear. She was green, blue, and purple—emerald-like facets of beauty. I began to talk to the little creature. This time, I said out loud, "Please, sweetie, I want to help you. I'm only trying to gently guide you to the door. Please, sweetie, let me help. I truly do know what's best. I'm not here to harm but to help you find true freedom. Come on, sweetie."

I could see her little chest gasping for breath; she was tired. And that's when it happened. She allowed me to place the broom just under her, and she hopped onto the bristles. She stayed perfectly still atop the bristles of the broom as I walked across to the doorway.

The broom served as a chariot and presented its emerald cargo to the outside. She took one glimpse of the clouds and sky. There was a gentle movement of a fresh breeze, and her wings lifted her tiny body into freedom. She chirped, this time of relief and joy. There was a tiny flutter, a blur of jeweled colors, and she was gone. I smiled as I considered the story she would tell her family. And then God spoke ever so clearly to my heart. "Did you get the message, child?" He asked.

"What message, Father?"

"The message of the hummingbird."

"There was a message? I thought it was just a good deed."

"There was a message," He said. "Think about it."

"Let's see." I began to reason. "The hummingbird was trapped, and I tried to help her out of her rather large cage. And that would be like me—trapped in some bondage to something. I flutter and fuss and try with my own reasoning and strength to find an opening out of my problem."

"Keep going," He said.

"And You gently 'broom' me along, trying to help me find a way out. But I think I know best, and I resist. I keep batting my wings, working myself up into a dither. The more I try, the more I tire. The more I tire, the more I fear. You want me to be free from my entanglement—one *I got myself into*. And you keep using that broom to guide me. But no—oh, no. I keep trying my own way and return to my roost of a chain to rethink my way out."

"You're doing pretty well," He said.

"And then the night comes. The darkness is touchable. I'm afraid and alone. There isn't even the broom to bring comfort. The monsters of the night—not dogs and owls but deep-rooted fears—prowl just below me. It is so dark, and the darkness is made deeper by the loneliness."

"You're going in the right direction," He said.

"Finally the dawn comes, but I'm weary—no food, no water, no one. The night of my despair has made me even more fearful. And then I see the broom again. My tightened throat finds a way to chirp out a fearful call. Perhaps someone will hear, but nobody does. I dart away, and then I hear Your voice. 'Sweetie, I'm just trying to help. Let Me guide you.' And finally, I have no more strength to fight. I risk a rest on the top of the broom. It feels good to be there. It's so much more comfortable than the chain. Perhaps I'll just stay there. There seems to be a little movement, but I'm content. And then I feel it—fresh new air. I tilt my head and see the trees, sky, and sun. My wings have new life, and I take off into the wonderful world You prepared for me—into Your freedom. It's much prettier than the cage."

"I think you have it," He said.

"Father?"

"Yes, child?"

"Thank you."

Then the Children Prayed

This is a story of heartache and tragedy that touches the most fragile part of us. This part never wants to see our children hurt, ill, or injured. Parents are determined to shield their sons and daughters from pain. This story will shake those of us who have or love children to our very core. This is the story of a child and the words that fell from the doctor's lips: "I wish I could tell you otherwise. There is little hope." This really isn't my story. I was on the outside looking in. But I am glad that I was allowed to look.

She was in the first years of elementary school, full of vim and vigor, precocious and precious. She had hair that fell in short ringlets of curls that were never quite in place but always bouncing. All the events around her home seemed pretty normal. A mother's instinct caused a phone call to her pediatrician. I'm sure the mother thought the words from the doctor's lips would be, "Nothing to worry about; you're just an overanxious mom." So Mom and daughter entered the medical office that was booming with well visits, bumped knees, and bee stings.

Her turn came, and she walked confidentially into the doctor's office. A quick and painless examination provided little outward evidence of the storm that would soon erupt into this young family's life. The doctor was extraordinarily calm when she stated, "Let's get an x-ray." When the x-ray was read, the doctor ominously said, "We're making an appointment for you with an oncologist." There was no time to wait or think—just immediate action. They got back in the car. The girl's three rambunctious brothers reacted as all siblings do: "*Yuk*—another boring doctor's visit."

The princess was taken for another examination and x-ray. Based on the findings, the new doctor delivered the message with medical precision; there was no way to make it any easier. A review of the tests showed that this precious little one had a tumor located behind her eye. There was very little doubt it was malignant. The mother's heart sank. She tried hard to listen to all that was said. They would do a biopsy within a few days to determine the type of malignancy and then decide on treatment. Because of the location, the tumor could not be removed. They would treat it. It was probable the child would lose her eye. It was possible, because of the rapid growth, that the prognosis would be worse. This was unimaginable. How many other parents had faced this? How many had walked this path?

A sleepover for the entire Sunday school, grades one through three, had been planned for that weekend and was just two days away. The kids were excited, as you can imagine. It was a sleepover in church with a ton of games, fun, and food planned. The mom and dad decided to allow life to be as normal as possible.

This little one had been carefully told that she was ill: testing and probably surgery would follow. Her parents wanted to prepare her for what was ahead. They had shared with friends that prayer was needed. This was no small thing they faced. This was the time to ask everyone to pray—and pray hard—that God would walk with them in these next days and months ahead. But for now, they wanted everything as routine as possible. As they said nighttime prayers with her, tucked her in, and read her a Bible story, a desperate thought crept in. Would this be the last time? Cold, dark, suffocating pain embraced the hearts of her parents. They were determined to shield her from those fears during the days before life would change. So with her sleeping bag under her arm, she left to enjoy an evening of fun with her friends.

The events of the evening were wonderful. There was lots of food, fun, giggles, and games. Toward the end of the events, before they began to try and sleep, the children's minister gathered them around to talk about Jesus and pray. With the parent's permission, he shared with the children that this precious little one had a medical problem and would go to the hospital in just two days. She would have an operation. Would they pray for her? Sure, they would. Without prompting, fifty little bodies rose, gathered around her, and laid their hands on her.

The children never questioned that doctors could be wrong. They never hesitated to ask for a miracle rather than asking for strength to walk through a difficult time. The children never hesitated; they only knew that God is who He says He is, and He said if we pray, He will answer. The children had learned to ask, and God will answer. There was no doubt; they would pray, God would hear, and He would answer.

They prayed such prayers as you have never heard—trusting prayers of pure faith. They really believed God heard them and that He would answer what they asked. *Heal our friend. Don't let her be sick or hurt. You can do it, God. So please just do it. Take away the bad thing that is inside of her, and make her all right again.* Around the room, tiny, trusting voices lifted prayers up to God with confidence that He would answer. They didn't rely on x-rays, doctors, or prognoses. They prayed in simple faith for complete and total healing—nothing less.

And so the next week came. The waiting room was crowded with family and friends and filled with prayers, heartache, and tears. They waited. The details of those hours are not important. It is enough to say that the doctor walked out with head shaking in unbelief. "Never have I seen anything like this before. I saw the growth. I snipped a small part for a biopsy. And like an ink-filled balloon, it completely deflated. It's… well… gone." The walls of the waiting room that had just been bombarded with tears, grief, sorrow now reverberated with yells, screams, and rejoicing. I imagine God smiled. How could He do less than honor the innocent, faith-filled, undoubting prayers of fifty little voices?

Some of us have prayed for strength to walk through difficult times or for healing, but I'm not sure we really believed it would happen. Our aha moments came when we realized that with the faith of a child, miracles do happen.

More than a year after that event, she is still free from any effects with the exception of a small scar from the biopsy. If you have a child or a loved one who has a diagnosis that is severe, please know that God's answers do not always come in such a dramatic manner. For those who have lost a child or loved one, my heart and prayers go out to you. God does hear. This time it was with an amazing miracle.

Abraham

She was just old enough to understand a little bit about life—not a child but still not yet a woman. In her world, a child became a woman when she was twelve or maybe thirteen. She didn't have enough of life's experiences to know that her family was poor. She knew that some people lived in large homes and wore wonderful clothes. She had very few clothes, and her family didn't live in a huge home. In fact, they lived in a tent. They raised a few animals. But she always had enough to eat, and she felt safe. Although her father was a bit stern and gruff, she knew deep down that he loved her. Her brothers teased her and played "keep away" and loved to hide (especially at night), jumping out to scare her. But she'd seen them intervene when the older neighborhood kids picked on her.

Her mother was the fussy type, always cleaning, cooking, and puttering about in the little bit of land she called a garden, but she loved her husband and children. Her mother believed in chores, especially for girls, and she was the only girl (so far) in the family. Her brothers got to go out with their father and have fun—they got to hunt, fish, and work with the animals. That was her favorite part. She loved animals. She wasn't allowed to have a cat or dog—foolish things that just eat and sleep, her mother said. But she loved the animals they did have—even the smells that weren't always so nice.

Each animal they owned had a purpose, her mother said. There were a few goats for milk, but they weren't friendly, and she was a little afraid of them. A few chickens provided eggs, kept some of the bugs out of the garden, and even provided a hearty meal every now and then. The donkey was assigned for hauling items and served as transportation when her father had to journey far from home.

Her favorite animals were the sheep. They weren't white and fluffy like some people thought they should be, but they grazed slowly and drank deep from the small area at the nearby creek where her brothers had prepared a rocked-off drinking area for them. Sheep won't drink from running water; the water has to be still. And the sheep, even the lambs, let her come up close and touch them.

She liked to talk to the sheep. They didn't make fun of her or run away, even when she asked silly questions. She had lots of questions. Some she didn't dare ask her mother or father. *How do babies get here? Why did God paint the sky blue? Pink would have been a better choice.* She had lots of questions about religion. She knew one thing about religion—it had lots of rules. There were many things you couldn't do. And she knew when you did something wrong, you had to make it right. She didn't do much wrong, but when she did, she knew punishment was coming. Talking after her father had said "Go to sleep" was a bad one. Or not obeying quickly when her mother told her to help with preparing a meal. She learned that rules were made to be quickly followed or punishment was a sure thing.

There were lots of rules. She'd seen her brothers get into *real* trouble for disagreeing with their father. And her parents always talked about sacrifices that had to be made for what they called sins—things that were contrary to the rules that God had given them. God had never given her any rules, but she could only imagine what would happen if she disobeyed one of them. Like the goats, she was afraid of God. He must be very stern and unhappy when people didn't carefully obey each and every rule.

Life was good. It was springtime. She loved it when the cold months were past and warmer weather came. Grass began to turn green again. The sheep could graze closer to home. Best of all, lambs were born. They were cute when they tried to walk and then when they learned to skip, bounce, and run. She loved being with the lambs. This year, it was wonderful—eight new baby lambs, four boys and four girls. She usually liked the girl lambs best, but this year, one of the boy lambs stole her heart. He came running in a crazy zigzag pattern and nudged her with his nose. He stuck out his head, and she scratched his ears. He made the softest sounds. She named him Abraham.

She was very happy when she saw her father telling her mother that "This will be the one." Her father said that Abraham was perfect—that he didn't have a single mark or blemish on him. She already knew that he was special. She spent as much time with Abraham as she could. He followed her, well, like a lamb. They walked to the pool of water together, and she watched him drink. She stayed nearby as he ate grass. He looked up every now and then to make sure she was near, and he'd make that quiet sound again—a sound that he would make only for her. It was their special language.

She overheard her parents talking one night at the table, and her father said that it was "time she accompanied them to their place of worship." She never got to go. First, she was a girl, and second, she was young. But this year, her father said, she should go with them. She dared not look up from her plate or even make a sound. Children weren't allowed to talk at the table. Many people in their area traveled to the city once a year, but she had never gone. She couldn't wait to tell Abraham. It would be their special secret—her very first trip away from home.

Her mother began to prepare food for the trip. Her brothers worked, storing and packing other things they would need for the journey. Her father got the donkey ready. The day drew near. She was so excited that she could not sleep. When her father left the tent, she asked her mother questions about the place they would go and what she would see. There were many things she wanted to know. Her mother finally told her to stop asking questions or she would be left at home. So she talked to Abraham. She told him all about the trip and what she thought it would be like to be in the city. She told him about the shops where they sold bread, cloth, candles, oil lamps, and perfume. She could hardly imagine what it would be like to see bread already made or what it would taste like.

She told Abraham that there would be lots of strange and different people. They would go to a large place called a temple to worship. In the temple, she and her mother would have to sit in a place away from her father and brothers. She knew that words would be read from prophets who wrote them a long time ago. She would get to see people in the temple from far away. Abraham ate quietly, turning his head every now and then to let her know he was listening. She hugged him and scratched his ears, and he stretched out his head to nudge her slightly; it was as close as he could come to hugging. He made that special sound that let her know he loved her.

It was almost time to leave when her father told her that they would take Abraham with them. She was so happy that she couldn't speak. Abraham would get to see it all too. How wonderful it would be to have Abraham go with her. She ran down to the sheep shed as quickly as she could to tell him. He ate a little hay, and she thought he smiled just a little. Now she would have someone to talk with as they traveled and someone to share all she saw. The adventure included her best friend. She hugged him tightly, closed her eyes, and dreamed of the journey.

The day came. Her family and many neighbors began the long walk. Her father got a rope and put it around Abraham's neck. She smiled. Abraham didn't need a rope. Abraham would follow her wherever she went—and that's exactly what he did. As they started down the dusty road, he simply walked right beside her, stopping every now and then to chew on a few clumps of green grass and then jostling to catch up with her. The rope dangled on the ground at his feet.

The city was a long distance, and they had to camp out along the way. It was fun. The family built a campfire, roasted meat, and saw all the other people camping nearby. She felt safe and very happy. For the very first time ever, Abraham slept right beside her. He was her perfect friend—the perfect lamb. He snuggled in, just waiting for the rest of the journey.

They finally arrived to the noise, smells, and sights of the busy city. People were everywhere she looked. She didn't know that there were this many people in whole earth. Tall people, short people. Some smiled nicely. Some didn't. There were men, women, boys, and girls and different dresses, and some spoke words she couldn't understand. Shops offered everything—fruits, vegetables, meat, and chickens; sandals, clothes, and oil; perfumes, candles, and sweet-tasting breads.

The next day, they would go to the temple. She was excited. That night, sleep was easy. She was exhausted, and Abraham was just what she needed to help her feel at home. The morning came. Her father came and took Abraham by the rope. She couldn't go with them, her father said. She would come later with her mother. She didn't understand, but she knew she should never question her father. As soon as they cleaned up the breakfast dishes, she and her mother began the walk to the temple. Today was the day. She would get to see what the inside of the temple looked like.

As she drew closer to the temple, the noise and the smells were almost overwhelming. There was a smell of fear in the air. Animals with ropes around their necks struggled against the pull that edged them closer to the gate. She knew that sacrifices were demanded by Yahweh and were needed to make the communication with Him continue. As they drew closer, her mother held her hand tighter. The crowds were compressed. The smell of animal sweat and all the mess that they make was almost choking in the hot, tight air. Despite the throng of people yelling at the animals, hitting them with sticks to make them move, pushing and shoving, she caught sight of her father and brothers. Slowly, with messy ooze coming over the edge of her sandals, she and her mother made her way toward them, inch by slow inch, bumping against the dirty fur of a goat or the tangled mass of hair of a sheep.

When they were closer to her father, she caught sight of Abraham. He stood still, not struggling between her brothers. The rope was limp, and when Abraham caught sight of her, he stretched out his head to reach toward her. She was very happy to see him again and pulled against the constraints of her mother slightly to reach him.

She wasn't sure exactly when all of it came together, but somewhere between the time she began her push toward Abraham and the moment she reached him, she realized exactly why he was there. The thought rushed over her like a wave of nausea. *Abraham. Abraham.* The perfect lamb, her father had said. She rushed to hug his neck. She clung to him desperately. *There must be another way. There must be something else.* Abraham looked up at her with trusting eyes of love. Then her brother pulled Abraham away from her to the priest. She didn't want to look. She couldn't bear to look; yet her eyes moved to the stones that made the altar.

The stones were drenched in blood. The blood ran down onto the dirt beneath—what she thought was dirt. It was soaked and wet. The priests stood up to their ankles in blood-soaked clay. As each animal came forward, the blood flowed even more. The linen garments of the priests were red, drenched in ever-increasing stains. The blood ran down their strong, muscular arms and hands that held the reluctant animals. The front of their linen tunics, the belts at their waists—everything was soaked in blood. The warm, oozing smell penetrated the air.

As she gazed, frozen in horror, Abraham moved closer to the priests. She wanted to scream. Her throat was frozen. And then Abraham was there. The priests tilted his head back, lifted the knife, and made one strong, swift movement. Abraham didn't make a sound. He didn't pull away. He simply looked trustingly at her, and with what she knew was unrestrained love, he simply relaxed. She hid her face in her mother's side and felt her mother's arm go around her shoulders.

She loved Abraham. It hurt so much that she didn't know if she'd ever breathe again. They turned and began the journey from the altar and the smells of death. Only when she gazed over her shoulder for a final look was all that it meant revealed. Abraham loved her enough to give up his life for her, to make her right with Yahweh. It cost Abraham. He gave up a wonderful home, green pastures, and a perfect existence and walked among the gore and dirt of earth. Abraham gave up all that he had for her. He had a perfect love.

Maybe, she thought, that was what God meant by all of this— perfect love, perfect sacrifice, perfect pardon, perfect reconciliation. Could the promised Messiah she heard of offer any more? She would never forget Abraham or his love—and she would never forget his sacrifice.

Christmas

The story of the birth of the God-man, Jesus Christ, the Messiah, the Promised One, has been told a million times. Many miracles occurred that night. Prophecies were fulfilled. There was a virgin birth. God confined Himself to the form and constraints of a human being a being He created. Angels said, "Glory to God. Peace on earth. Good will to men."

Think back to that time. Mary was a young teen of perhaps twelve but no older than fifteen. Joseph was older but totally devoted to his bride-to-be. She was the envy of many who watched this little girl as she began to develop into a young woman. They saw her heart full of desire to serve Jehovah. They knew of her caring and parental submission. And they knew she loved this man named Joseph.

Then it happened. News spread like wildfire. Mary was pregnant and unmarried, the father perhaps a despised Roman. Joseph was crushed. His very manhood was called into question. His parents were angry. They begged him to rid himself of her. His heart was broken. Since their betrothal, he had waited, planned, and built a home for her, and he loved her still. What could he do? How could he stand this injury to his soul?

At Mary's house, the scene played out was one of bitter disappointment, and her parents were beyond despair. Some man surely must have forced himself on her. Hadn't they warned her not to go see her cousin Elizabeth? What foolishness. She was a sweet daughter but so naïve. They told her the city was wicked. And now—the news, the neighbors, the relatives. For a fleeting moment, their thoughts turned to Joseph and his embarrassment, but those thoughts quickly returned to their own plight as her mother wept with tears flowing over her cheeks. Her father stood with hands clenched, tears flowing not across his cheeks but across his heart.

Pause now and go to another place. Travel with me to the threshold of heaven. See now the Father embracing the Son. The Father said, "I send you to the earth, where hatred thrives, where Satan and his demons roam. I send you to the beings We created. You'll know firsthand the effects of disease, jealousy, hatred, deceit, and betrayal."

The Son looked at the Father and spoke words that echo through the corridors of time. "To teach them love, I must go. To teach them how, I must show. They have no way to come to Me; I'll pay the ransom to set them free."

Looking once again, we see Joseph and Mary as they traveled from their home to the tiny hamlet of Bethlehem. The decree from the Roman emperor came harshly on the heads of the people except perhaps Mary and Joseph. The decree allowed them to flee from the harsh words, whispered messages, and cold, unforgiving glares of their neighbors. After the long journey, traveling dusty roads, fearing robbery or worse, they found themselves in Bethlehem in a manure-filled shed. But they had each other, and they clung to the promise delivered both by the angel and the prophets of long ago.

Soon, the crisp night air was punctured by birth sounds. Joseph's inept hands, rough and calloused from his carpentry work, helped birth the Messiah. The newborn was tenderly placed into a feeding trough. Exhausted mother and relieved husband both gazed in wonder at this tiny God-king. They watched in amazement, wondering why God chose them. They were awed as the God-king wrapped his tiny newborn hand around a finger and fell soundly asleep. Jesus, a baby, confined in the bonds of human flesh, began to grow. He cooed "Abba" when reaching for Joseph. As He took His first unsteady steps as a toddler, echoing in the distance, you can still hear those words if you listen carefully: "To teach them love, I must go. To teach them how, I must show. They have no way to come to Me; I'll pay the ransom to set them free."

Months passed, and the wise men visited. The light they saw was the Shekinah glory of God. The angels were simply awed by what was happening, and God cracked open the door of heaven, allowing them to see what was unfolding on earth. From His heavenly throne, the Shekinah glory illuminated the night sky of the shepherds and wise men. As the wise men got ready for the trip, they began to pick out gifts for a king. These were not small gifts. They would travel a long way, so it had to be a worthwhile visit and memorable gifts. After all, this was a king they were traveling to meet. They had been directed by that heavenly glow. This was the time to pull out the big credit card, get the big gift, and rent a large camel.

Jesus may have been two years old by the time the wise men arrived. We know because Herod had all boy babies from newborns to two years old killed. We also know Joseph and Mary were in a home. We can imagine that Christ was still breastfed by His mother. The practice was to wean a child at two. There were no expenses for Him—no disposable diapers, just rags that were washed. No food had to be bought. He would have slept alongside His mother and stepfather, so no bed was needed. Toys were a few pieces of wood Joseph had left over from a carpentry project; they may have become Jesus' toy blocks.

Joseph was the perfect stepfather. He too had been chosen by God for the amazing role of step-fathering the Messiah. But God was not about to abdicate the duties and responsibilities of a father. God simply would not allow another to shoulder what a father should do in providing for His Son. No way. Enter the nobles—the kings of the Orient—and their gifts.

A chest of gold was for a king; gold was the surefire thing to give. It was to recognize the *position* of the person. It would provide food, clothing, and care for God's Son. (He wouldn't need health insurance.) God made sure that His Son, the Son He would provide for while He was here on earth, would not be the responsibility of another. Joseph, I'm sure, would have willingly taken on that support, but God said, "Thank you, no. I will provide for this Son of Mine as I have provided for you. Take this gifted gold, and use it wisely to care for Him." I believe that the last nugget of gold was used the last day Jesus was home—when He left the home of his parents and began His ministry.

A chest of fragrance was given to a king, for He should smell like one. The smells of the Bethlehem manger may still have been fresh in the memories of Mary, Joseph and Jesus. But this God-child should live and smell good and the fragrant gift brought new memories. I'm sure Mary used it sparingly. She may have used it to barter. I imagine she gave some away from time to time to widows, the needy, the hurting, and women who had few if any people to share woman things with them. As Jesus walked down the street as a toddler, as they traveled to Egypt and back again, and as they settled in Nazareth, people would pause and turn as that hint of fragrance lingered near this little one. As He grew, I'm sure some of His memories were the smells of His childhood—Egyptian clover, baked bread, freshly hewn wood that hung about Joseph, but perhaps the most captivating was that of frankincense. That was unique; no one else had a home that smelled like that. As Christ grew from toddler to manhood, there was a fragrance about Him; all sensed it even after He left a room. This gift recognized His *presence*.

A chest of myrrh was also given. Myrrh comes from the balsamaceous shrub (think of balsamic vinegar) and is a brown aromatic gum resin with a bitter, pungent taste. It was often used to embalm as it helped to contain the smell of a decaying body. But it was given to a King, a newborn. Perhaps this was a tradition of the Orient, and these kings recognized that death is a part of life.

But Mary, the one who "kept these things and pondered them in her heart, (Luke 2:19" somehow knew deep within that the gift of myrrh would be used. Her mother's heart silently screamed. Her stomach tightened and knotted. She would hide this gift. She would not think of it for the time being. Perhaps she would never need to see it used. She would save it as a dowry for her Son. (She imagined marriage as the usual process in His life.) It was an unusual thought—a dowry for a Son. But perhaps His bride would use it. Somehow Mary sensed this was the most needed and practical of all the gifts. (His bride would use it, but Mary could not have foreseen that bride would be both Jew and Gentile, and she would be the church.) Although this is something we won't know until the scroll is unrolled and read in heaven, I wonder if Mary, as she knelt at the foot of the cross and watched her Son die, now knew that last chest, that dreaded gift would be unlatched, released, and used. And perhaps this was the spice used and placed on His body as He was placed in the tomb.

The last gift, the gift of *procurement*, was used to purchase you and me and is offered to purchase anyone who will simply look to Him and say, "Yes, Lord. I'm yours for the purchase. I'm yours. But You knew that as You hung, tortured and dying on that cross. You knew already; as You died, You whispered my name. I can hear in my mind's ear those words coming from your parched lips: 'I love you, child. I'm doing this for you. I'm giving My life so you don't have to give yours.'" Hear again those heaven-whispered words: "To teach them love, I must go. To teach them how, I must show. They have no way to come to Me; I'll pay the ransom to set them free."

The gold was a wonderful gift and represented His position. The frankincense was valued and represented His presence. But the gift of myrrh that represented His procurement was the ultimate gift of love. Have you received His gift of myrrh? Have you offered to share it with anyone? Do you have the fragrance about you? The offer is extended. There is no more pretending. It's time to get real. It's a time of myrrh.

Feet and Fragrance

As more candles are added to my birthday cakes, I've found it is harder to take care of my feet. I began to think about the feet of Jesus. As with all mothers, I'm sure Mary counted His fingers and toes after He was born. This was her first baby, after all, and she wanted to make sure all of Him arrived. Given the unusual circumstances of His conception, I think she must have wondered just a bit what God's child would look like. Would He have wings? Would He have a strange, glowing halo encircling His head? Would He have toes, or was there something else that God would use to walk? What about fingers? Perhaps He would feed Himself in some celestial manner. If I were Mary, I'd have counted His fingers and toes. It's just a motherly thing to do.

I love little baby feet. The babies don't seem to know quite what to do with them, and the big toe is often the best thumb they choose to put into their mouths. Mary was no different than any other mother. She washed those pink baby feet. She may have counted on His toes "one little lamb, two little lambs…" (They were Jewish, so she wouldn't have called them piggies). You can imagine how she watched as Jesus toddled His first steps. How breath-stopping that must have been—God walking on toddler feet! I'm sure she watched Him jump into mud puddles after a strong Nazarene rain, as any seven-year-old boy would do. Perhaps Joseph gave Him a bit of wood left over from some carpentry project. Perhaps Jesus carved that wood into a tiny ship complete with a sail. Mary watched as Jesus waded into the water, toes sinking down into the mud, and launched that toy ship on ripples that resembled waves. As they walked to Jerusalem, she smiled as she noted that those feet had grown significantly larger and now made footprints in the dirt – footprints so much larger than her own.

I'm sure she watched with pride as He entered those teen years, knowing that He would soon face His bar mitzvah. She knew He'd do well. He always did in His studies. She watched with eagerness as He became a man, walking with humble confidence down the road, leaving home, launching into manhood. She saw the puffs of dust erupt from the road as He began His journey. She kept all those footprints of memories etched not only in her mind, but also her heart—the feet of Jesus.

When a young Jewish boy finished his education, he would select a rabbi (teacher) under whose umbrella of learning the Jewish boy wished to be. There were no graduate schools, so the boy, by now in his late teens, would go to the rabbi whose teaching he most respected and ask, "May I follow you and learn from you all that you can teach me? May I put your yoke (cloak) of learning on my shoulders and learn?"

The most wonderful statement anyone could make to that young Jewish man was, "May you walk so closely to your rabbi that you will be covered in his dust." Oh my! In my mind's eye, I see Jesus walking the dusty roads and paths of Israel. I see the dust puff-up in tiny clouds as the throng of people crowd around Him, especially His disciples, pressing-in close to get every word and thought. As they press in, they become covered in His dust. What a thought.

The sanitation of that era wasn't great. Both animal and human excrement found their way onto the walking paths. Rotting food, decaying animals, and the most foul-smelling components of life were underfoot. only a thin sandal protected the feet, and those sandals did only a modest job. Sharp and jagged rocks cut through the leather. Feet were dirty, bruised, cut, and usually in some state or process of healing. The feet of God walked in human filth, and so Jesus walked among us.

Our culture differs significantly from that of first century AD. Those who were mentally challenged or simply the lowest on the social roster were relegated to the task of feet-washing. When someone entered the home of a noble person, the foot washer would quickly appear, bowl and towel ready to wash those filthy feet that oozed with germs and contamination. The servant would remove the sandals of the visitor as the visitor made himself or herself comfortable and then the servant would carefully wash the feet, getting between the toes to remove all the filth and creatures (like bugs) that had accumulated. The homeowner certainly did not want that filth being tracked onto the Oriental rugs and contaminating the home. When the feet were washed, the dirty towel was rinsed and hung out to dry, and the bowl water was thrown out into the street so that someone else's feet could get dirty.

Jesus entered such a home, but no servant met Him. He simply wasn't noble enough to have His feet washed. But then, as Jesus sat to talk to the homeowner, a woman whose reputation put her at the bottom of the social register entered. There was a stir in the crowd. The conversation continued; it didn't even slow down. Perhaps as she inched her way through, some thought it was just the foot washer finally getting to Jesus. Perhaps others saw that it was only a woman and ignored her. Others may have recognized "that woman" and moved away from her lest they be contaminated by touching someone like her.

The woman found her way to Jesus. She bent down with great humbleness, as she too knew who she was and what she'd done. She gently removed His sandals. From the folds of her robe, she brought out a precious box, opened it, and poured the contents on His feet. Not water but perfume. Everyone was watching. The fragrance wafted up, filling the room. The conversations around the room ceased; there was a deafening silence.

What would Jesus do? Did He know who—what—she was? The very expensive perfumed oil washed over His feet. There was no towel. Did she forget to bring one? Her long hair pinned up on top of her head and under her scarf, was released in a cascading flow as she removed the pins holding it in place. The hair covered her face, and she bent low, allowing the lockets of her hair to absorb her tears and the ointment as they became one. The room was silent except for the slight sounds of sobbing, as she continued to caress the feet of the One who showed her complete acceptance, unbelievable and unconditional love.

Let's leave that room and come back three days later. The perfumed oil permeated the rug and the area beneath it. Take a deep breath; can you smell it? Now go with me to the marketplace. There's a woman who walked with a basket on her arm. A long scarf covered her hair, and as she looked at the items for sale, her face was barely visible. Lamps were for sale at this vendor, material at another, and leather for sandals at another. She exits one market stall and enters the next. There was a wonderful fragrance in the air. No longer could you smell the pungent animal odors or the recently caught fish, but you could smell the wonderful fragrance. Inhale deeply, and you'll catch it too. She must be the one—the woman who just three days ago poured perfumed oil on the feet of Jesus. Of course, the scent still remained in her hair, which she used to dry His feet.

Nearby on a hill just outside Jerusalem, Jesus taught. He shared what He called parables as He strove to teach the unenlightened audience simple truths. About Him remained that same delightful fragrance—a reminder to Him that there were people who loved Him. This reminded Him that the path He faced would be incredibly difficult. Perhaps the humanness of Him laid claim to the comfort that there was at least one who poured out her adoration. He cherished the fragrance of love and adoration. Perhaps, just perhaps, it would make the rest of the journey a little easier. Perhaps as He made that final, agonizing walk up Calvary's hill, He would for a fleeting second recall that fragrance.

The fragrance once poured out lingered where it was poured. In that room, in that place, many inhaled the wondrous aroma that day and in days beyond. Even after His crucifixion and resurrection, that aroma remained, reminding them that those in the room had met the Messiah. At least one woman had touched Him (John 12).

This fragrance is in the adoration we pour out to Him. It remains on us and on those we meet. As I pray, it is why I sit at His feet and why a vital part of the time I spend in prayer is time spent pouring out the perfumed oil of adoration to Him. I hope that others may inhale a bit of the fragrance of Him that lingers about me.

No Room

So much work, these travelers—ah, men. Caesar issued a decree in his great wisdom: "Each man shall return to the city of his ancestry, and there he will apportion to Rome's treasury an amount of tax to be determined by the magistrate." And my husband, son of Abraham that he is, had a brilliant idea. We will open our home to the weary traveler and fill our hands with their coins—yes, that's what he said. And in they came with their dirty feet and the smells; some smell worse than the camels and donkeys they travel with. There was not a place in our home for another sleeping mat. The dirt and the noise they make, even at night—the snoring ... you should see the size of the noses on some of these men. Oh, the snoring. Who can sleep? But Haremiah is never one to turn away a shekel or even denarii.

Just a few nights ago, I wiped the last crumb of bread from the table. The weariness of these old bones was finally placed on my sleeping mat—and there it was, another traveler knocking at the door. Haremiah did not even rise from his mat; he simply bellowed, "Go away; no more room." Again the knock; again the response: "Go away; no more room." But the traveler was persistent. Haremiah threw back the bedclothes and with a bit of anger unlatched the door to face the one who interrupted his sleep. "I told you, there is no more room."

I went to stand beside him to add my voice should the traveler try to enter. I saw a dusty man standing there; like all the others, he had no choice but to follow Caesar's decree. And then my gaze drifted down to the woman at his side—no, not a woman but a mere girl, and she was with child. She leaned wearily but confidently on her husband's arm. She wasn't beautiful, but there was a certain glow about her—more than just the glow of one with child—that made its way beneath the dust of the road to display itself on her face. I struggled within myself to explain what I saw. She had a purity of look, serenity, peace—that was it, a look of humble peace, as if she understood more than her young years should allow. I heard the man imploring, "My wife needs a place to rest. Please, sir."

My husband's gaze softened; perhaps he was thinking of his own daughters. But his words, although they were uttered a bit softer, remained the same. "There is no room in this place for you."

I gave him a wifely nudge and spoke directly into his ear. "Let them have the stable out back. It will provide some protection from the chilly night air, the straw a measure of warmth, and since it is close to our home, a measure of safety as well."

Haremiah began to shake his head but turned to the man and said, "We have nothing more to offer but the stable out back. It has straw that will provide some softness for sleep, shelter from the night air, and a place of some safety for you and your wife. Stay there if you like." The man eagerly shook his hand, and the wife smiled; my husband took a lantern and guided them to the stable. When Haremiah returned, I squeezed his arm. He grumbled as he again lay down on the mat, but it was a pleasant grumble. I could not sleep. Perhaps just the events of the day caused this sleeplessness. I thought of the young girl, soon to deliver a child. I remembered those days when I was like her, anxious, excited but very afraid. I could only hope she would have someone near to comfort and help her with the birth. I hoped she would have an easy birth. I prayed Jehovah would grant her a male child as her firstborn.

I had been awake for many hours, but the sun had not risen when I heard sounds of many rustling feet—whether from men or animals, I could not tell. I gave Haremiah a good nudge, but he only moaned and pushed more deeply under his coverings. *Might as well investigate this myself,* I thought. I got up, wrapped a cloak about me, and went to the window opening. There were people gathered at the stable. It was one thing to allow the young couple to rest there but if others had been summoned to stay, they should pay. My heart was a bit soft for this young mother-to-be but others should pay to lodge. I would see to this matter myself.

I went outside in the predawn of the day. The men were shepherds, and they smelled worse than those in my home. What were they looking at? I quietly got closer. Finding room enough to look between two of these men, I followed their gaze, and there in the feeding trough was a tiny babe. Why, that young girl had her baby. The new mother rested on her elbow, her hair damp from the process of birthing. The babe lay peacefully asleep, swaddled in strips of clean cloth, tired as well.

The husband stood proud and protective, wiping his hands with pride. Men do not assist in birthing. That is a women's job; yet he had been the only one there to help. His hand moved down to touch the cheek of his wife. She reached up to touch him. They looked knowingly into each other's eyes.

But why were the shepherds here? As if my unspoken question had been heard, the shepherd nearest me leaned down and spoke. "We were in the fields; the night was brilliant. Stars hung in the sky like jewels; the sheep were resting. We sat—all of us—beside the fire for a bit of warmth. Without warning, a brilliant figure appeared. I will admit to terror. I was shaken, not knowing what this was.

"The being spoke: 'Don't be afraid; I bring you good tidings of great joy for you and for all people. To you is born this very night in Bethlehem, the city of David, the Messiah, as Jehovah has promised. Get up; go see where He is. Search until you find Him.' And suddenly the eastern sky was filled with brilliance and angels who said, 'Glory, glory, glory to Yahweh.' It was over; the sky returned to smooth velvet blackness with only the stars for light.

"We gazed at each other, and we came to the stable here. We found Him just like the angel said—the young girl and the Messiah. Just as the prophets said. We are the first to see Yahweh's promise to Israel."

I cannot tell you how much longer I stood there with the shepherds, but then we moved as one and began to leave to tell others the events of the evening. The Messiah had come. We went throughout the village of Bethlehem telling everyone we saw. The Messiah had come. Yes, oh yes, the Messiah had come.

Pedicure

I am probably one of only a few women who had never had a manicure or pedicure. My feet are not works of art, and I really did not want to display my toes to another. But when I was finally persuaded to undergo the procedure, it felt wonderful—the warm water, the gentle massage of my lower legs, ankles, and feet. The women who gave pedicures worked diligently. I never saw them motionless; they were always working, cleaning, arranging, or dusting. And they performed their tasks with great dedication and diligence. All went well the first time. I left with fire engine-colored toenails and clear polish on my fingernails. (I wasn't ready to reveal to the world how wild I was so I kept the loud color only on my toenails.)

The next time my daughter asked me if I wanted to go for a pedicure, I was ready. Things went well. The massaging motion of the chair I sat in, the soaking feet, and the gunk of the dead skin removed from my heels all left me luxuriating in comfort. A few days went by, and my toe felt funny. I took a quick look at it. Nothing seemed to be out of the ordinary except a slight pink color of the skin. After a few more days, my foot let me know that something was definitely wrong. Shoes of any type hurt. I sat myself down, pulled my foot up to rest on my knee, and took a good look. I didn't have to look too hard. The area around the big toe was inflamed; it matched the fire engine red of the nail polish. I touched it gingerly. *Ouch.* Even the slightest touch was painful. I remembered the scale in the hospital with the happy to unhappy faces that help you try to describe your pain. I gave this one an eight.

I debated what to do. To try and examine it further was not a good option. *I'll ignore it,* I thought, *and it will simply take care of itself. Probably a small cut.* That settled it. I wouldn't think about it anymore. Another day went by, then two. It really hurt. For such a small thing, it made a major impact on my quality of life and even my quality of sleep.

When a few more days passed with no improvement, I hoisted foot onto knee again. It was not any redder than before, I calculated. *I'm going to let it go one more day.* And I did. But by the next day, it was obvious something would have to be done. I plopped myself down, hoisted foot onto the knee again, and with tweezers and nail clippers, I explored the area. There it was—a tiny bit of toenail that had not been removed, and it was digging into the toe. *This is going to be bad,* I thought. *I'm going to have to yank it out, and the pain will be horrible because the area is so tender.*

I gritted my teeth, placed the tweezers on the offending piece of nail, positioned myself so that if I passed out I wouldn't fall too far, held my breath, and yanked. It came out without any protest. I think it was glad to be released, and my toe was certainly thankful to have it gone. A few days later, the redness had diminished, and all was well. That's when the quiet voice of God spoke lightly to me.

"Child, did you get the message of the toenail?"

"God, I know you speak in wonderful ways—but the toenail?" I didn't seem to get a message."

"Think about it. Walk through it with Me."

"Okay. I had a pedicure, and a little bit of toenail was left that began to hurt."

"Good job," said God. "Keep going."

"Well, it was irritating, and I looked at it, but I didn't do anything."

"Why?"

"Because I thought it would take care of itself—you know, work its way out."

"Did it?"

"Well, no. It got worse."

"Did it hurt?"

"Yes, even though it was very small, it impacted all of me, disrupting my life a little."

"So what did you do?"

"I looked at it again. I thought about taking some action, but I thought it would hurt."

"And did you?"

"No, I left it in, but it got worse."

"What did you do?"

"I gritted my teeth and removed the little bit of toenail. And I felt much better."

"So," said God, "how is that like anything in your life?"

"Oh. I get it. I have a little sin, just something small that irritates my spiritual life. I keep looking at it, knowing I should do something. But I don't. I think it will just, well, go away. And then finally, when I can't ignore it any more, I sat down and yank it out."

"And," asked God, "did it hurt?"

"Not nearly as much as I thought it would. Just a quick moment and it was over. And then I felt better."

God smiled. (I could hear it in His voice.) "Well done, child. Keep up the good work, and next time, don't wait so long to take the action you know you need to take."

"God?"

"Yes, child?"

"Thank you for healthy toes."

Cold, Gray Rain

My husband and I had been married more than a few years. We'd survived the usual financial issues that couples face and weathered a few of the adolescent years with our children. We both enjoyed our careers and moderate levels of success. We were doing okay—nothing spectacular. Perhaps the fireworks of our romance were gone, but we had nice glowing embers and were both fairly young. We were moderately active in our local church, and in addition, I was working on an advanced degree.

Each weeknight, I came home after work, fixed a hot dinner, and we quietly enjoyed it. Homework was next while my husband read the paper and watched whatever sport was broadcast. Something deep inside of me sensed that things weren't just quite right. We had a good marriage, I thought. The occasional spat might occur but nothing extreme. Neither of us gambled or drank, and the strongest drug we used was a protein drink. But every now and then, there was the chill that made the hairs on the back of my neck stand up. I'd shake it off and continue to display the outward portrait of a perfect household, family, and couple.

This night was like a thousand others. We both came home from work in our separate cars. Tonight it would be just us at dinner. He settled in the family room to read the paper while I prepared the latest dish I had discovered in one of my magazines. The table was set, food was served, and my husband was summoned to dinner. We said grace—a fairly routine process with memorized words. As I picked up my utensils, I casually asked, "Seems like you've got something on your mind. Is everything okay? Is something bothering you?" *Good wife,* I thought, *asking about his day and his concerns.* I fully expected him to rattle off some difficulty at work or a personnel issue. But he didn't.

His words cascaded out as if some mighty reservoir had opened, spilling out urgently. The exact words don't really matter, but it was all there. He wasn't happy. Our marriage was not fulfilling. He needed out.

I listened. Time froze. Surely I must have misheard. This man with whom I'd shared so much and who I thought I knew so intimately was telling me the world I had built was crumbling.

As a counselor, I have a particular voice I use to keep things calm and under careful control. You may not believe this. I heard that voice coming from my lips—calm, collected, portraying wisdom that I didn't possess. I told him that I understood. How could I sound so calm when I was screaming on the inside? I would like to be excused from the table to go in the other room and consider all he had said. I thanked him for his honesty, suggested that we needed to decide how to move forward, asked him to think about what we should do, and left the table.

I walked in zombie-like fashion and placed myself on the end of our loveseat. *Ironic,* I thought, *loveseat.* I rehearsed again and again all that he had said, looking for an out, desperately wanting a solution. That's what I was trained to do—evaluate the problem, find a solution, offer it, and move on. The more I contemplated all that had occurred in the last few minutes, the angrier I became. How could he continue to sit at the table and eat the meal I had prepared?

Why wasn't he in here with his stomach in knots? Why wasn't he working to solve the problem? But he didn't; he finished his dinner. I heard him leave the kitchen and go to his home office. I cleaned up the table and washed the dishes. The kitchen looked like it had just a few hours before—perfect. Everything was in its place, but what looked right was anything but.

The next days and weeks passed by as we worked out the details. The Christmas holidays were approaching, and we needed a plan. He moved out and into his own apartment. The house seemed cold and empty. We did all the legal things we needed to do. But we didn't tell anyone—not family, coworkers, or church members. It was all fairly easy to handle. When he didn't attend church on Sundays, the explanation of work issues was given and easily accepted. I didn't have to say much. "Oh, you know how busy work can get at this time of year." I didn't really say he was working; I just suggested it.

My performance at work received rave reviews as I began working more hours to avoid going home. Home wasn't home; it was only a house. Projects at work that were scheduled for completion in the spring of the coming year were wrapped up before the end of the year. Even the CEO of our company stopped by my office late one night to chat about how much was getting done.

Except for the immediate family (those living at home), we didn't see other family members often, and concealing our situation was not too difficult until the holiday celebrations began. I'm not sure how we worked it out, but we went to social events as if we were still together. Our communications were very limited, but somehow details were shared. The church's Christmas party was at 7:00 p.m., and we both showed up, driving separate cars, entered together, met and greeted others, and laughed and ate. At some signal between us, we said goodnight, walked out together, and then separated to our individual cars and lives, having never spoken during the entire event. This same scene played out time and time again at different social events during the holiday. We never missed a cue. No one suspected. We were very good at roleplaying.

Christmas came and went. The new year began. It was different than it had been twelve months ago. But as God removed so much from my life, I began to rely on Him. I read my Bible more and claimed Ecclesiastes 3:11: "For He hath made everything beautiful in His time." My old fifth-grade English lessons served me well. That's a future perfect verb tense. It does not say God will make but that He has made—already accomplished it. One cold, gray January evening, I was leaving work, late as usual, driving in the bleakness of the cold night. I began to cry, a luxury I did not often allow myself. As I drove and sobbed, I cried out to God, "I don't know how You are going to make this thing beautiful. But I believe You. You don't lie. So I am claiming that verse as my promise from You. You will make this beautiful."

At that moment, I gave it over to God. I didn't know exactly what that meant. Perhaps God would give me the strength and peace to walk alone. But I was determined to let God be God and just trust Him. (It seems silly, doesn't it? It is so simple and yet so hard.)

How it all happened after that night would take pages to fill. God, in His infinite wisdom and mercy, rewove our marriage. We both had made mistakes. We both needed a loving Father to forgive us and help us. We did go through some marriage counseling. I resolved that I would never mention the issues that had caused so much pain. We resolved to forgive each other and build a stronger marriage. If you asked my husband years after this event if our marriage was better than it had been, I think he'd smile that unique crooked smile of his, shake his head, and say, "Yes—oh, yes. It is much better."

Does God work the same way in every situation? Absolutely not. There was only one burning bush, and that was uniquely for Moses. God is creative and has a unique plan for each of His children. Each plan is tailored not only for the person but to bring Him glory. After all, the whole purpose is to do just that, bring Him glory; we are just privileged to be part of the process. Consider your situation, whatever it is. Apply Ecclesiastes 3:11 to it. God will make this thing beautiful in His time.

Timeout

I know this may not be the correct way to handle things. It was a few years ago when our guidelines were not as strict as they are now. I worked with a children's group, and some of those children were classified as handfuls. They had lots of energy. Either their parents hadn't taught them much about obedience or the children just hadn't learned those lessons.

On this particular day, one little girl was acting her worst. When asked to join the group for a game, she went to a window and removed the blinds—just pulled them down on top of herself. And then she jumped up onto the windowsill. She was quite nimble, petite, and agile enough to escape hands that tried to protect her. Many times, the same scene was repeated. "Come on, let's play with the parachute games." She was off and running. I knew her mother well enough to know that she'd want us to do all we could to keep her in the group. And I knew that I would not have any concerns if I needed to speak more firmly to her.

One of the other workers finally had enough. It's interesting when that moment of "enough" arrives. Taking her by the hand, the worker escorted the little girl, about five years old, to me. "She needs a timeout," said the worker, and she placed the girl in the chair nearest to me. The worker left and the little girl quickly jumped up out of the chair

I had every confidence that the mother would approve of my actions. I quickly grabbed the little girl's hand and brought her back to her timeout seat. As soon as the hand was released, she was up and darting to get away. This was all a game to her. So I brought her back again, this time to my lap, and placed her right in front of me with my arms casually around her. When she tried to escape, I simply tightened my grip, relaxing that grip when she ceased to try to get away. We watched the other children laugh, enthralled in their play. She was quick, waiting until she thought I wasn't paying attention, and would make another attempt to escape. My arms tightened; she pushed at my hands, now held with fingers intertwined. She didn't cry; she simply tried to get out. Many minutes went by. Then she said, "This isn't fun."

"I know," I said. "Sure looks like the other boys and girls are having a lot of fun."

"If I were home, I wouldn't have to sit here," she announced.

"You're right," I confirmed. "If you were home, you would be by yourself and not have any friends to play with. It really is sad that you can't play with your friends tonight."

She mused that over for a while and then stated, "This is boring. I'm bored."

"I'm sure you are," I told her. "Sitting and only *watching* are not nearly as much fun as playing and running." She tried to open my fingers. I ignored her attempt and just sat and watched, making an occasional comment to the other boys and girls about how well they were doing and cheering them on.

"I want to get down," she said. This was as close to an apology as she was willing to make.

"Sure," I agreed. "You know the rules, and as soon as you tell me you are sorry for the way you behaved, for not listening to Miss Nancy, and promise me you will behave, you can get up." No way.

She tried unweaving my fingers again and pushing my arms. And then she sat quietly for a minute or two.

"I'm sorry," she said. "I am sorry I didn't listen, and I promise I will play nicely." I gave her congratulatory hug and released her. I am pleased to let you know that not one other incident occurred during the remainder of that year. (I did share with her mother what had happened and how pleased I was. The mother readily agreed.)

And then, there it was—God's voice. "Child, do you see how much like that little girl you are?"

"Me!" I responded, "Me! I'm nothing like her."

"Want to think about that some more? Give it a try."

"Okay, let's see. She didn't want to listen. She wanted to have fun her way."

"Good job. Just like you," said God.

"And I keep getting myself in trouble and in danger of hurting myself. And You remind me to get back with the group; that's where the real fun is—and its safe there, too. But I won't listen."

"Keep going," He said gently.

"Finally, you place me in a timeout on the sidelines. I can watch others enjoying their Christian walk, having all the fun, while I'm stuck. I notice that when I rebel, though, You hold me closest to your heart. Your mighty arms protect me even though I keep trying to escape. You hold me near your heartbeat, just showing me that You love me. Until…"

"Until what?" He asked.

"Until I can see where I was wrong—where I was in danger, where I can see that what You had planned for me was more fun than what I was doing. Once I sat still, in Your lap, You let me see that others were enjoying You and having much more of a good time than I was by myself."

God said, "I think you've got this lesson. Now, get on out there and play."

Baaaa

I was praying one day. "Lord, show me where You want me to go, what You want me to do. Just let me know what the next few chapters are. I want to be used by You. I want to be used in some way."

And Father said, "Are you a sheep?"

"Yes," I said proudly. "I am your sheep. Can't you hear me as I *baaa*? I have wool that can be used. Or I can chomp down some grass. I want to be a sheep that has a job to do. Show it to me, and I'm on it like a lamb on clover."

Father smiled indulgently. (I could hear it in His voice.) "Sheep, when I take out my flocks to graze, drink, and rest, I never tell them where they are going. They trust Me. They don't need to know where the pasture is for the next day's food. If I gave those sheep a book of My plans for them, they wouldn't be able to understand all that was written. They'd lose valuable time and energy trying to figure out tomorrow rather than just grazing the grass of today."

"Oh," I bleated.

"So, precious sheep," Father continued lovingly, "do *you* trust *Me* enough to let Me take care of the pasture for today's grazing and rest securely in the fact that I have wonderful pastures for tomorrow and the next day?

Slowly, I grasped all He said. What else could I say but *"baaaa"*?

Tokens of Love

My husband is not romantic. A dinner by candlelight is usually met with a comment like "I can't even see what I am eating." But he delivers true moments of pure joy. I like to think that he's not a gigantic Hershey bar but more like Hershey kisses that pop up in the most unexpected places.

I don't often travel alone, at least not to any locations that are a great distance from home. Usually it's a family trip, or if business-related, colleagues are my companions. This particular January, I was scheduled to travel to Des Moines, Iowa, for a business trip, but no one would travel with me. With my roots firmly planted in warmer soils, I'm not much for cold weather. January was not a month I wanted to be in the northern Midwest. Iowa is a lovely place, but I'm not a great fan of snow unless I'm beside a fireplace watching those on the slopes.

As the time approached for me to leave, I began to carefully watch the Weather Channel with a focus on Iowa. The weather channel indicated temperatures in the thirties—that's the daytime high—and lots of snow. My plans now incorporated warm sweaters and socks. What if I was stranded due to bad weather? What if the winter storms knocked out electricity? Survival became a consideration—or at least keeping warm enough to feel like I was surviving. I packed what I'd need for business purposes and included items I could layer in order to keep warm.

I shared a quick kiss with my husband, practiced over our twenty years of marriage, and gave him a final look as I boarded the plane and he saw me on my way to Des Moines. Not until I reached my hotel room late that night and began to unpack did I find those special items that he had carefully placed in my luggage. The first was a knitted snow cap—not something I usually have in my wardrobe but that my husband uses when he shovels snow. He's not one to quickly throw out a useful item, so this one was very used. The signs of age and many hours spent working outside in the cold were evident. But there it was, with all of its pulls, snags, and faded color, carefully tucked into the side of the suitcase. The message was loud and clear: *Just in case you get stranded, this will keep you warm.*

Digging just a little deeper, I found four packages of nabs somewhat the worse for wear and travel—and more crumbs than cracker—but there they were just in case I got stranded in an airport and there was no food available. And because he knew my sweet tooth, three little snack-sized chocolate bars were at the very bottom of the suitcase.

These were not diamonds, a new car, or even a dozen roses. But they were treasures, unexpected little gifts of love. And that's what it's all about—watching and caring, taking the time to pack a treasured snow cap, sneak in a pack of nabs, and tuck away a tiny chocolate snack. I sometimes think that the marriages of today that struggle are those in which one or both partners don't know how important a simple snack-sized chocolate bar can be. It's not the big things but those small treasures that are important. Not a big house or a luxury car, not even membership at a country club or diamonds presented in a lovely box—just a small chocolate bar or a frayed snow cap. I didn't need to wear that knitted snow cap,

Aha Moments

but I did sleep with it beside my pillow that night right after I ate a snack-size chocolate bar.

God does that, too. He presents us with big surprises but also tucks in small aha moments of wonder and amazement.

Prognosis: Miracle

My husband and I entered the phase of our marriage in which life was getting comfortable. Empty nest—*ahh*. The mortgage was paid off. *Ahhhhhh.* We had both worked long and hard and were virtually debt-free. The holidays had ended. Decorations had gone up and come down, and were now nicely packed away for another year. Family had been over, and better still, had left. We love them, but returning to the quiet routine of our lives was just fine with us. We had married in our twenties, and our marriage had grown to the stage where the embers glowed warmly—not so much like a roaring fire but that gentle, bone-warming time of life when you know just when to stoke the fire and when to let it provide warmth. We had weathered some storms and were now comfortable with each other, even in the quiet moments of conversation without words.

We often discussed plans to take a long vacation and travel cross-country, perhaps for a month or so—Alaska or maybe even a little travel outside the US. That would be a big step for my "I love America and America only" husband. We discussed what the next chapter would hold for us. A short-term mission trip was certainly in the offering. We were excited about the opportunities that we would have to enjoy each other and just be together.

January began with my husband continuing to battle a persistent cold and cough. He put off going to the doctor, as husbands often do. He had a slight case of walking pneumonia the year before. I encouraged him to see a doctor, and he finally did. They took an x-ray and gave him a prescription. That was on a Tuesday. On Wednesday morning, the doctor's office called and advised him that he needed to see a doctor for more testing. My husband said his schedule was too busy. The nurse strongly encouraged him to follow up immediately.

I was at work when he called, He was more agitated that his plans would have to change than he was concerned. He wanted me to get him out of this. With permission permitted through federal and medical guidelines (HIPAA), I called his doctor. I was told something had shown up on the x-rays, and it needed immediate action. An appointment was made with a specialist that very day. That should have been an indication to us that this issue was serious—and it was. A shadow around the aorta indicated the presence of a tumor. My husband was tall, thin, and in good health, and we were certain that surgery, at the most, would be all that was needed to take care of this issue. Additional specialists and more testing were scheduled, and within forty-eight hours, we had the diagnosis. Cancer became a very real issue in our lives.

My business experience had brought me into contact with doctors that I knew were the most respected oncologists in our area. I immediately began talking with them to set up appointments. Action filled in the areas where fear wanted to gain ground. We would fight this. We would win. Despite my best efforts, the insurance policy provided through my employer did not allow us to see the doctors we wanted and so desperately needed. Our only option was to go to a teaching government hospital, and so began the red tape that is often present in this type of facility. The urgency of before was replaced with more steps, more doctors, more "You must see this doctor, then do this, then go here." Days turned into weeks, and weeks became months.

We never questioned the competency of the medical staff, only the time it took—time we were losing, as no treatment had begun. We got referral after referral, testing and more testing, but no treatment. We trusted them, kept every appointment, showed up on time, and complied with every request, but still no treatment began. Because of the delay, a serious medical issue occurred, and hospitalization was immediately needed. A semiprivate room was the only room available. The other patient in that room was from the state prison and had been diagnosed with terminal cancer. Those hours with that man added much to my life, as he shared his story and even offered to share his meal with me. Surely, I reasoned, God had allowed us to be here for such a time as this. Less than forty-eight hours later, a medical student advised us that my husband's condition was stable and we could go home. But there was still no treatment and we were now approaching three months since the diagnosis.

We returned home, and in fewer than twenty-four hours, his condition plummeted. I called the teaching hospital, talked with the medical student on call, and was told we needed to immediately return. He asked me to hold for a moment so that he could arrange an admission and advise where we should go. This is one of the largest hospitals in our state. It is huge, and while some of the other area hospitals may go to 95 percent occupancy, this government-owned facility almost never does.

The student doctor returned to the phone. "We have an issue here. It seems all the beds in the hospital are occupied. Do you live near…" He named the hospital that was closest to us. I gave him an affirmative response, and he asked if we could go there instead. Could we? My husband's condition was rapidly deteriorating, and the fog was so thick that driving would be a challenge. To be directed to a hospital closer to home—not the thirty-five miles we had been traveling—was wonderful.

I helped my husband into the car. I would learn later that he was totally unaware of what was happening and did not even recall the drive to the hospital. His condition was serious. Before I pulled out of our garage, I paused and had a word of prayer with him. I asked God to safely see us through the fog and to the hospital for the help we so desperately needed. Then we began the journey—not so much to a hospital but on the path where God would reveal Himself as powerful and passionate, a God who takes care of His children. Weather was rough, and visibility was not more than several feet. I inched my way down the rural roads to a major highway. There were still several miles to go. I drove slowly, praying each mile that no one would hit us in the pea soup of the cloud in which we traveled. A cloud engulfed not only our car, but also my heart.

We made it. The lights at the emergency room entrance were barely visible in the wet shroud that blanketed everything. Admission papers were completed. My husband was taken into the examining room and they asked me to stay outside. A young doctor came out. He apparently had yet to take the course in how to keep calm in a crisis. His demeanor was one of anxious dread and his tone high-pitched. Did I know what my husband's pulse oxygen was? Did I know that he could not survive at this level? Would I sign papers to put him on life support? There was no time to waste. "Hurry, do it," he instructed. Why, he asked, hadn't I taken him for medical help before now? It was probably too late. There was little they could do.

Trying to absorb all that he said was almost too much. As calmly as I could, I assured him we had been seeing doctors for almost three months; we had just been admitted and discharged from another hospital before my husband's condition worsened, and then we were sent here. He left me, stating he had to get back to see what he could do. Time passed. A specialist—in fact, three different specialists—was summoned. They questioned me about the delay from diagnosis to now—why there had been no treatment. I explained all that we had undergone for these past months. I was advised that we now had the very doctors we had initially wanted. Doctors who were initially denied by the insurance company were the doctors handling my husband's admission. I offered a quick prayer, thanking God for filling up those hospital beds and directing us there. I felt relief and peace. Finally, action was being taken.

The next days saw no improvement, and his condition was critical. I spent my hours in the intensive care (ICU) waiting room or his room when I was permitted to go in. Wires and tubes kept him alive. The medical staff, nurses, and doctors were wonderful and kind, although their looks told me the situation offered little hope. My husband and I had discussed life support. He would agree to this medical procedure but only for three days. He had five specialists addressing his many issues that were caused primarily by the delay in treatment we had experienced before this team took over. One of those doctors came to the ICU waiting room to talk with me.

"Your husband," he advised, "is probably not going to survive. We have a last-ditch effort we want to make. There is a new surgical procedure we would like to try." There was only one doctor in the area who had been trained in this new procedure—and that was the doctor I was talking to. Regrettably, he advised, one of my husband's lungs had completed stopped functioning, and the other barely worked. His condition was so advanced that the nonworking lung was gone and could not be resuscitated. They hoped to improve the condition of the other lung. He was kind but straightforward in advising that he held out little hope that the surgery would have a good result. In fact, he did not think my husband would survive the procedure. Could they proceed? I said, "Yes, please. Thank you." He advised they would schedule the procedure the following morning.

I went in to see my husband, who was in a medically induced coma. Although he had no way of hearing me, I shared with him the plans for surgery. When the diagnosis was originally given, he had claimed a Bible verse: Isaiah 41:30. "They that wait upon the Lord shall renew their strength, they shall mount up on wings as eagles, they shall run and not be weary, they shall walk and not faint." I repeated those words quietly to him as I held his hand tightly. It was the same grip I used to hold myself together. Many minutes later, I kissed his cheek and said goodnight.

I hadn't been home in days and needed both a shower and some sleep. What I hadn't shared with anyone was my growing fear. I was afraid that the surgery would not be successful and that I would have to walk alone. But over all of that fear was an almost certain knowledge that we had no medical coverage for the doctors who were treating him. I drove home in the very late hours of Wednesday night, went inside, and pulled out our medical insurance manual, reading even the small print. It was much as I thought. We were without coverage for all that was being done. The doctors, five specialists now, were not covered under the insurance plan. After a quick shower, I went to bed. Sleep was impossible.

As I had done so much during the last months, I began to pray. "Lord, what am I going to do? The bill is probably in excess of $300,000 and growing. You know my checking account doesn't carry anywhere near that amount. Lord, what am I going to do?" In the early hours of the morning, I called the ICU and spoke with the nurse. I explained that I did not have insurance coverage or cash, and I could not let them proceed without advising I could not pay for all that was going to occur.

She was compassionate. "Dear," she said, "you have far more seriously important things to think about. Come in tomorrow, and I'll get social services at the hospital to help you." That means you will meet with a social service representative of the hospital, and she or he will help you work out a payment plan. More than $300,000 would have to be paid to the hospital. I thanked her and hung up.

Sleep continued to be impossible. I began to pray as I had never prayed before. I don't know how long I prayed, but I got to a point where I finally said, "Lord, I will remortgage our home, use all of our savings—it's only money. I am going to trust You to provide what we need. Let me live a long time so that I can repay what I will need to borrow. If I trust You for eternity, I need to learn to trust You for today." I felt an overwhelming sense of peace, as if a very warm flow of air began at my head and swiftly drifted down across my body to my feet. I felt totally at peace and at ease. I breathed a "Thank You, Lord," rolled over in bed again, and closed my eyes. Two hours later, I woke up, refreshed.

I got up and went to the hospital to see my husband before he was taken to the operating room. He would remain in his bed, as he was too critically ill to place on a gurney.

While I was with him, my daughter came into the ICU and advised that the social service rep had come by to see me. I knew I needed to sign those papers and shoulder a debt that was extremely large and growing by the minute. I left the ICU as soon as my husband was taken down the hallway to surgery. My daughter stopped me. "No, Mom," she said, "the representative said just to give you a message." Certain that the message was an appointment to meet with her, I asked what time the appointment was. "Not an appointment," said my daughter, "just a message."

"And the message?" I asked. The message was that the bill had been paid. I knew my daughter was anxious over all that was happening, although I hadn't shared the issue of the uncovered hospital costs with her, and was certain she'd gotten the message wrong. I asked again and got same response; the bill had been paid. I immediately went to see the social service rep, convinced that the message had been relayed incorrectly. The rep was very kind. I asked about the papers I needed to sign, and she advised, "There is no remaining balance; the bill has been paid in full."

She continued to explain that a representative from my insurance company visited their hospital only once a month. That visit had occurred the day before—Wednesday. The insurance rep pulled only one file, my husband's, and across that reviewed file wrote, "Paid in full. Do not charge the patient the deductible. All will be covered" followed by a signature and the date. I asked to see the file and was shown exactly those words written across the top page. All of it, even future costs with unauthorized doctors—every penny, even the deductible, was paid. I asked for a copy of that page just in case someone changed his or her mind. In a daze, I thanked the social service rep and left.

As I walked down that hospital corridor, God spoke to my heart. "Child," He said, "did you notice that I sent the insurance rep to look at just one file and on the day *before* you prayed about this? You see, child, I love you immensely more than you can imagine. I had the problem solved. I was ready to tell you the moment you turned it over to Me. Today is Thursday; you turned it over to me early this morning."

God continued His message to me. "I was so excited that I could hardly wait for you to get to the hospital so you would know all I had done." I leaned against the wall of the corridor, cried, prayed, and thanked God for loving me and taking care of things. My aha moment had come. I learned that if I had asked Him on Tuesday rather than waiting for Thursday, He would have had the answer ready to take care of all my anxiousness. I promised never to forget what He did that April day. And He stands ready to do that again for me—and for you.

Winning a Battle

After the miraculous issue with the hospital bill, I faced the long hours waiting for a report from the surgeon. He came to the ICU waiting room still in surgical garb. He shook his head in a negative manner but said, "I just don't understand it. We were able to easily take care of what was needed." (I'm leaving out the details, as they are very unpleasant.) "And after the surgery was completed, not only is the lung we were working on operating as it should, the dead lung is back to 50 percent plus." I told him I understood it—that I had a God who was right there in the operating room, answering prayers. I thanked the doctor for the part he had played in this second miracle of the day.

Because of all that God had done, I was able to face the days ahead with renewed trust and confidence. Many more days in ICU, intubation removal, and my husband's slow recovery saw us moved from ICU to tertiary care. We were unable to leave the hospital floor due to monitoring devices he wore, but we could at least see outside and watch as winter's bareness turned into the fresh green of spring. As with many who have been cooped up, my husband longed to get outside of his room, so I placed him in a wheelchair, and we rolled down the hospital corridors; only one floor was permitted. We decided our task was to pray for the others in the hospital. We'd roll up to a room, read the name of the person on the doorway identification tab, and pray for that person. Then we'd move on to the next room. It gave both of us a sense of being useful in an environment that needed our prayers. After more days and more healing, we were finally discharged.

It felt wonderful to be home again. We were in our own bed, at our own kitchen table, and eating home-cooked meals. (I'm not that great a cook, but at least we were home.) Eventually I was able to return to work, making sure he had all the care he needed. The improvement he made was amazing. We began to get invitations to speak to groups about our walk with God. I enjoy speaking to groups; my husband did not enjoy this as much. We worked out a process where we'd walk to the platform, he'd introduce himself and then me, and I'd take the microphone to share what God had done in our lives, especially over the last few months. I believe God lets us walk through issues so that we can provide a helping hand and words of encouragement to others who have just begun a similar path. That's what we found as we traveled and spoke to groups. Some audience members were hurting and needed to know God was there for them.

We told them that we began this particular chapter knowing that God is faithful, and we saw a magnificent display of that faithfulness. Amazingly, when we turned to the last page of the chapter, we saw those words written as the closing sentence: "God is faithful." We were delighted to share all that had happened. I can't count the number of people who came to us to talk about their own situations. We cried, laughed, and prayed together.

The Next Chapter in Our Life Book

A year after the hospital event, my husband continued with chemotherapy that went very well. The side effects were minimal. Then we had the doctor's visit at which we expected continued good news that he was well on his way to remission. The doctor entered the room with his nurse. Both looked somber. As calmly as he could, the doctor gave us the news; the cancer had metastasized and was now in the brain. We asked what was next. My husband needed six weeks of intense radiation to kill the cells at the new site. We took a deep breath and clung to the promise that God is faithful.

Radiation began. During this time, we were asked to return and speak to the very groups we had spoken to almost a year earlier. Our presentation this time was a bit different. We relayed the first story very briefly and told them we had read those words at the end of that chapter: "God is faithful." And a new chapter began. We wished we could say that the cancer was gone, but it wasn't and had found a new site. But we assured them we were a bit smarter this time. We had flipped some pages forward and read the last words at the end of *this* chapter of our lives; those words were "God is faithful."

We moved forward with calm assurance that He would handle this chapter as well.

On Tuesday morning, my husband seemed very lethargic, and I made a call to his doctor. "Bring him in immediately," I was told. "We will have a team waiting for you."

I called our daughter and asked for help in getting her dad to the car. She said, "Mom, haven't you learned? Call an ambulance. They will be able to do a much better job." For this admission, we were not allowed to return to the hospital where he had been in the ICU but (due to insurance again) had to go to a medical facility about forty miles from our home. I got a bag of his hospital necessities ready to go, called the ambulance, and waited.

Our daughter arrived simultaneously with the ambulance team and provided them with information. They were very kind. I traveled behind the ambulance in my car so I'd have transportation available to return home once he was admitted. We took the entrance ramp onto the interstate. My cell phone rang. *Strange*, I thought, *I don't give my cell phone number out to many.* It was an odd time for anyone to be calling. The voice was a deep baritone. "How are you doing down there?"

"Fine," I answered, bewildered. Who was this?

"Are you sure you're okay?"

"I'm fine." I had my sunroof open and looked up to see if I saw anyone in the clouds. I thought this was going to be one heavenly conversation.

Then he identified himself. "I'm the paramedic in the ambulance ahead of you. Your daughter gave me your cell number. I need to let you know that your husband's heart rate has soared almost off the charts. By law, we must immediately divert to the nearest hospital. We wanted you to know." So much for my heavenly conversation.

No problem. The nearest hospital had all of the medical records from the many weeks we spent there. It was our hospital of choice! As we pulled into the ER entrance, the attendant said, "As soon as we pulled up to the ER, your husband's heart rate returned to normal, but we are going to ask for an emergency admission." A quick check in the ER identified part of the problem as dehydration. They would admit him for overnight palliative treatment, run some more tests, and release him the next day. After a twelve-hour wait in the emergency room, we were admitted. Once admitted, I planned to go home and get some rest and return early the next morning.

The details aren't important, but God firmly closed door after door when I tried to leave. I would try the door again, and God's hand held it closed. He seemed to say, "Child, I want you here." The doctors had indicated that given the current course of his illness, we could expect another ten months or so before his condition would be terminal. They held out little hope for complete recovery. I prayed for another miracle.

The night wore on. I had a wonderful chance to talk with our nurse and share with her the God that I had come to know so intimately. She listened, thirsty to have something she could believe in. She had seen so much suffering, so many deaths, and so many lives shattered. She said she had never wanted to work on the oncology floor but felt drawn to this area. I prayed with her that she would have a peaceful night and thanked the Lord for giving her to us. She squeezed my hand and left the hospital room.

This was our sixth hospital admission, and I was quite accustomed to sleeping in chairs. My habit was to place the hospital chair facing my husband. I would then hold his hand, lean back in the chair, and hope that sleep would soon come. This position allowed me to see his face immediately when I opened my eyes, and if he woke up, he could see that I was there. If he needed me, he only had to squeeze my hand. It also allowed me to quickly view the monitors that were behind the bed, and by holding his hand, I knew if he made the slightest movement. I closed my eyes and began to pray, as I had so many nights before. This time it was a bit different. I sensed that we were about to begin a new chapter.

Until this time, the invasive disease had caused discomfort but not much actual pain. For that, I was very grateful. I mentally made plans to obtain a hospital bed, as my husband seemed to rest more comfortably in this one. Since I felt our path was moving to more serious issues, I planned to request a leave of absence from my employer; I had already been offered one, and the company had been very gracious over the last months. With those two issues mentally settled, I began to pray.

I prayed for a long time and tried to go to sleep. God seemed to whisper in my ear, "I want you to be awake tonight just to be with Me." I had only had a few hours of sleep the night before and should have been tired. Sleep would not come. So I prayed some more. I prayed for everyone and everything I could think of—every government official, church member, relative, and on and on. The medical staff at the hospital was wonderful, quietly coming in to check on us, noting information, and quietly leaving.

Around 4:00 a.m., I sensed a need to pray for something along a different line. I told the Lord that I knew He could be glorified through suffering. When we go through difficult times and evidence our trust in Him, He will see us through the tough times, and others will see Him through us. That led me to pray for strength. I told Him I knew how tough the path of suffering could be—for the one suffering and loved ones who watched that suffering. I asked God to allow us to walk through the suffering and glorify Him. But, I asked, on the morning of the day when the suffering would be more than could be handled, more than I could bear to watch, to please take my husband home at the dawn of that day—the morning of that day when the suffering would become too much.

I sensed a little movement and opened my eyes, adjusted my husband's hospital sheets and pillow and whispered some encouraging words. "The doctor will be here soon; they're going to run some tests." I wasn't sure he even heard. I rubbed his arms and legs and then positioned myself back in the chair as he quieted down. I felt a strong need to pray that same prayer for strength through suffering and God's release on the morning before the suffering would become too great.

As I opened my eyes, I noted the predawn brightness making the once invisible cars in the parking lot visible. Again, I felt a slight movement and rang for the nurse. I'm not sure why, as the issue did not seem critical, but I rang—something I rarely did. My husband, who had not spoken or moved significantly all night, raised his right arm. He inhaled deeply and said, "Help me, Lord. Lord, help me." And he exhaled. I waited for him to take another breath. After all, he had been breathing for years—but there was nothing.

I went to the hallway, saw a nurse, and said, "I think I really need you." She came in and announced that he was gone. She also called our nurse. They asked me if I wanted a few minutes alone with him. I did.

I prayed and thanked God for the years we had had together, being with us, and seeing us on our path. I thanked Him for answered prayers. I then thanked my husband for all the years he had put up with me and told him I loved him. Then I said, "I think heaven is a huge place. So when I get there, let's meet on the corner of Hallelujah Boulevard and Amen Avenue." I kissed him good-bye and opened my eyes to see that the sun had risen.

Our nurse stood at the door. She said, "I've seen many moments of parting, but I have never seen one like this." I shared with her that my God was able to provide a peace that I could not explain but could only experience. We had a wonderful few minutes as I introduced her to a God who loved her.

The task of calling family and friends began. And the chapter closed, but at the end were those three words written again: God is faithful. And He was. On that morning, just before the sun came up, He answered my prayer. He kept me at the hospital so I could see the transition. It was a very special and solemn aha time. I asked Him for release on the dawn of the day when suffering would become too much, and He released my husband. God seemed to whisper to my heart the words He had spoken to my husband, "Come on home, son. I want you to see where the sun is coming from, not where it goes to." And God stood up, opened His arms, and welcomed His child home.

Saying Good-bye

Those who have experienced the loss of someone know the path is not easy. These next few lines are not meant to minimize that path of loss, grief, or pain. But a memorial service can be a celebration of all God has done. My husband loved the choir. He had a voice that sounded good in a group. He wasn't much of a soloist, but our choir director gave him a spot every now and then on a Sunday night. My husband would practice for weeks. He wanted to give God his best. There were two songs he dearly loved. The first had a slower rhythm but carried an awesome message, and a second was tremendously upbeat.

To begin this service of celebration and remembering all that God had done for us, my daughter suggested that we play a CD (recorded at our church) of her dad singing that message-packed song. At the end of the song, he had invited others to stand with him and sing—and that is exactly what we did. There were few dry eyes among the five hundred who attended. Our emotionally charged voices joined in singing a commitment to follow the Lamb. Then the choir sang the more upbeat song. It was a wonderful time of rejoicing. We are privileged to have great musical talent in our church. One particular man sings not only with great talent, but also a heart full of passionate love for the Lord. He sang that day, displaying amazing, sincere devotion. We had a time of rejoicing as our pastor relayed the many instances of the miracles we had experienced over the last months and all that God had done for, with, and through us. Then he shared that God wanted to do the same for those gathered that day.

The same God who walked with us through those shadows is waiting to offer you His peace, love, and presence. If you don't know Him, He's waiting. If you do know Him and have a personal relationship, He stands ready to provide His peace in whatever circumstance you find yourself.

Near Miss

Traveling to my job, a one-way trip of about thirty miles, required me to face quite a bit of traffic. I have strange rules that I live by, and one of those is that I allow myself to use a costly (toll) expressway only once a day, either going to work or returning home. Since I was much more anxious to get home in the evenings, I used a longer and slower morning route. I left home very early to avoid the traffic and arrived at my office well before others. I used this time for devotions and prayer. No one was there that early; the office had the eerie but comforting quiet that only an almost vacant building can have. I prayed for my coworkers as well as our CEO. If the CEO had a problem, we all had a problem.

In the evening, I'd wait until the initial rush of traffic was over and leave about an hour after the office closed. This was the time I allowed myself to use that wonderful expressway, making the commute time less than half that of my morning trip. On this particular day, I zoomed along as traffic flowed nicely. The sun was low in the western sky, and I accompanied the radio as a contemporary gospel song aired. God is good. I often attract waves from truck drivers and others when I put my hand up in the air as I sing and worship, which they mistake for a friendly wave. No harm is done to either of us.

The traffic was heavy but moved along nicely. Just as I crossed the bridge with the speedometer indicating I was doing every bit of speed the law allowed, I needed to get in another lane, saw an small opening, and quickly merged from my lane into the other. As soon as I did, I realized the cars in front of me were completely stopped. There was no time to look or even brake. I was going to rear-end the car in front of me doing at least sixty-five miles per hour. An arrow prayer (those prayers that are shot straight-up to heaven) went up that I would at least not seriously hurt the people I was about to hit.

I had no choice but to reenter the lane I had just left. Bumper-to-bumper traffic, moving fast, had quickly filled in the spot I vacated just seconds before. Maybe I would not do as much damage to those as I would to the cars in front of me. There was no time to signal or look. I simply turned the wheel, reentered the lane, and waited for the impact. I knew at those speeds, I would be hit multiple times.

I prayed again. "Lord, I can't survive this; please let my death be quick." I realized that I was still traveling fast but had not hit anyone… yet. And then I had a chance to look briefly around me. My decreasing speed made that only barely possible. I had removed my foot from the accelerator—still not braking, as that would have been catastrophic. There were no cars around me; there was an island of emptiness in a sea of fast-moving cars. Exactly how God moved all of those cars out of the space I needed to enter, I'm not sure.

I took the very next exit, as I found myself in the exit lane, where traffic is usually backed up and even slower, and exited. I found a side road and parked. I needed to let my heart rate lower to something within reason, but more importantly, I needed to thank Him for being there, catching the prayers, and having my guardian angel clear a path before I even knew I needed it.

Then I wondered how many times God had done just that—seen the predicament I'd gotten myself into when I failed to pay close attention to what was going on around me and provided a clear path of rescue. I had an aha moment. I spent more than a few minutes on the side street, thanking Him for taking care of me that day and for the days He'd done the same thing but I had failed to notice.

God is on our side. God is for us. God is for me—that makes it much more personal, doesn't it? And He is for you. He watches, cares for, and takes care of you each day, even during those times when you don't know it. The lesson here is to slow down, watch what is happening around you, and be aware that God is always in control, making a way of escape.

Diamonds in Brown Paper

I've heard that diamonds are often packaged and mailed in inexpensive brown paper to disguise the valuable content that is actually contained within. Sometimes events in our life are much like those packages of diamonds. To the outside world, there seems to be little of value in the dismal events that occur in our lives much like that package wrapped in crumbled brown paper. But, inside the package is a secret—diamonds—not revealed until the package is opened. The secret of the Lord is with those who reverence Him (Psalm 25:14).

After the harrowing year and a half of all that had happened during my husband's final months of battling cancer, I walked alone. I didn't like the word *widow*, so I considered myself to just walk alone. A major issue occurred in my life that was unavoidable and significant. The details don't really matter, and I'm certain many others have had situations occur that seemed insurmountable. This was one of them. I searched my memory and asked acquaintances, trying to find someone who could help in an area where I lacked any knowledge or expertise.

Several years before, my husband and I had engaged the services of an entrepreneurial group whose company had a biblical-sounding name. The work they performed was well done and I contacted them again. The individual, Kris, who headed up the company, was cordial with Southern genteelness. I was impressed by the personal interest taken and attentive manner given to the issue presented.

After defining all that needed to be addressed, the difficult decision was made to proceed with what I hoped would remedy the situation. I signed the contract and faced no small amount of debt. Kris and I established a nice working relationship, and I was very impressed with the other two individuals who comprised the employment base of this small company. The issue went well, the job was done, and the bill was paid. I wrote a note of appreciation to the team, and the matter was closed. Then several weeks later, difficulties were presented that evidenced all was not well. I called Kris, and we worked through some tough times to rectify the issue. In the process, we moved from a business relationship to one that was more friendship-based.

Christmas approached, and I purchased a small gift to express appreciation to Kris for remedying not only the first issue, but also for correcting the misstep that had occurred. In turn, I received a visit on Christmas day with an unexpected but heartwarming gift. I was especially touched by such a gracious gesture—a thoughtful gift delivered on Christmas day. There were some follow-up business issues that needed to be addressed, so early on a Saturday morning, we scheduled a meeting, and I had a country breakfast waiting. It was a pleasure to have someone to eat with and to see that person enjoy a meal.

More follow-ups occurred during the weeks and months, and more meals—sometimes breakfast, sometimes lunch, and then, if the appointment was scheduled in the evening, I'd prepare dinner, which we'd enjoy over long conversations and many cups of coffee. The bonds of friendship grew.

Weeks and months turned into a year, and we shared personal and business issues. My experience in business, public relations, and human resources allowed me to voluntarily help out in Kris's small but growing business. It was nothing much—just small tasks that took a considerable amount of time, and I had the time to invest. I sent letters to past and potential customers, and as Christmas approached again, I sent cards with handwritten notes to many clients.

One of my delights was dog-sitting for Kris's large lab. I'm a dog-lover, and this dog was a delight. He loved to fetch. His favorite item was a three-foot-long two-by-four. I would throw it until my arm throbbed, but this special canine brought it back until he finally laid the stick down and inhaled the contents of his large water bowl. He plunged his entire head as deep as it would go into the water bowl and inhaled. Water went everywhere. He was a delight. As I saw how this lovely animal so willingly and openly trusted, I felt I was making great strides in doing the same thing.

These tasks provided a welcome change from the demands of my position, and I enjoyed helping out. Kris and I had an occasional dinner and shared all the things that were happening in our worlds. The relationship was one of doting aunt to favorite nephew. A month had elapsed since our last dinner, and I received an e-mail from this adopted nephew. I opened the e-mail with excitement. I treasured our friendship, and it was good to receive a communication. I wondered what the next chapter would be. Little did I suspect as I read a five-sentence e-mail that the last sentence would contain the phrase "end our friendship." I read the three words again. I had envisioned our friendship continuing for many years. I had even taken steps to purchase a wedding gift I was going to give. Perhaps I misread the e-mail. I read it again: "end our friendship." Why? What had I done that would cause a severing of friendship? I responded to the e-mail in two sentences: "I am glad for you. My sincere wishes for much future happiness."

That was it. I had trusted, and the issue had ended abruptly and coldly with an e-mail. Not a visit or a call—just words sent through cyberspace. What had I done wrong? How had I offended? I rethought those lines in the e-mail and focused on the word "end." I mentally reviewed every recipe I had cooked, every letter I had written to clients, every card I mailed to customers, and those many times I dog-sat. I looked for an issue that would have caused a cessation of friendship. I couldn't find any, and I couldn't ask.

I cried, prayed, and reviewed even more. "Why, Lord? Why at this time in my life—why? Why allow the hurt? How can I get past this to trust anyone—to even trust You again?"

And God said, "Child, I know you are hurt. But this was necessary. I want you to consider that people may disappoint you. People may fall short of your expectations, but child, I promise you that I will never leave you. I will never give you any reason not to trust Me. I want you to look to Me for your direction. Child, do you think you can trust Me?"

With red-rimmed eyes, a snotty nose, and a quivering lip, I responded, "Yes, Father, I can trust you. You've never failed me. Through it all—every issue of life—You've been right beside me, always waiting for me to look to You for direction." And I ran back into the arms of the One I had drifted from, the One who loved me, who I could always trust.

I closed that chapter and much like those packages of diamonds, I found that while the outside was crumbled brown paper, inside was packaged a wealth of sparkling joy. And I walk more closely now with the One I know I can trust.

I'm Late

With an educational background that involves psychology and a challenging job that provided opportunities to assist people, I was often able to see a heartwarming end result. Using what I learned not only in the classroom, but also in daily experiences, I enjoyed volunteering in sometimes tense situations. That was where I found myself on a particular afternoon.

As I traveled from my office, I heard the traffic report; the route I would normally travel was deadlocked because of a multi-car accident. When critical personal issues are involved, being late is not an option. I often arrive early to set up, pray a little, and prepare myself for what may be a confrontational couple of hours. No problem; I'd allowed myself plenty of time to arrive early. While the change in travel plans would not allow me to arrive before the scheduled appointment, I wouldn't be late.

Others apparently had heard the same traffic report and were using the alternate route. My trip over the bridge was particularly slow and traffic was very heavy. I was still on schedule. Finally, on the last part of my journey, with ten miles to go, I turned onto a side road that allowed no passing and found myself behind a driver doing twenty miles under the posted speed limit. I sent the driver a mental message advising that I was going to be late and to please hurry or at least turn. No luck—apparently, telepathy did not work. With no other choice, I began to pray.

"God, this is going to be difficult. I am volunteering, You know. It is a crisis situation. Being late is not an option. Please move the car in front of me out of the way." No luck. We crept through three miles. I looked at my watch a hundred times, willing the hands to move slower. There wasn't even a way to contact the individuals to tell them I had been delayed. For six miles, we traveled at snail speed. Finally, we got to a traffic signal where I would soon be on a road that would allow me to pass. The light changed, I accelerated, and that's when I heard what sounded like a gunshot. I looked around quickly but did not see anyone with a weapon. Then I heard what sounded like a loud motorcycle roar behind me. My rearview mirror revealed absolutely nothing. The roar, but no more gunshots, continued. It took me a few more seconds to realize the roar was coming from my car.

I pulled over onto the hard-surfaced side of the road. Not knowing what else to do, I walked around the car. My right front tire had exploded, looking as if a small bomb was placed on the inside. Rubber and wire protruded from a large, gaping hole. The sound of the explosion was the gunshot I heard. The tires were almost brand new.

I called for auto assistance, and the man quickly came. He looked at the tire "Lady, did you see this?" Yes, I assured him, I'd seen the flat tire. "Lady, did you hit something?" No, nothing. "Lady, tires simply do not explode like this. Tires exploded like this many years ago, but now it simply does not happen. You have a defective tire. How fast were you going?" Twenty miles *under* the speed limit. "Lady, you outta be glad you weren't traveling any faster. If you'd been on the expressway or even if you'd gotten to the next road, where the speed limit was higher, and this had happened, you'd have at least flipped your car and probably hit other people. Lady, are you lucky."

I began to think. What if the tire had blown out at any other location? If I'd been on the bridge, traveling at any speed at all, I'd have hit someone for sure and would have blocked up traffic for hours. If I hadn't been behind that very slow driver, I'd have left the road, hit the ditch, and then probably collided with the trees that lined the roadway. And if I had gone any further than a couple of feet after turning, I would have accelerated—and who knows what would have happened. If the tire had blown out anywhere else along my route that evening, there would not have been a hard-surfaced shoulder to pull onto safely.

All along, while I'd complained, God was saying, "I'm protecting you. You don't know it yet, but the accident on the expressway, slow alternate route, and a really slow driver were all in place to slow you down so that you could safely pull off the road when this happened. Don't you get it? I'm in control. I am taking care of all of this." And as if that wasn't enough, after the tire was changed and I got to my appointment, there was a note waiting for me that the individual I was to meet would be an hour late.

God is in control. Aha—even when I can't see it. Even when it seems everything is going wrong, He is taking care of even the smallest detail. Just like He made sure I'd have a shoulder to use to safely pull over.

We Need Rain

There hasn't been any rain in a long while. The ground's dry—really dry. Streams are down to hardly any flowing water. We need a good, heavy shower and a soaking rain to water the grass and feed the streams.

I want to talk about the dryness. There's a lot of dryness everywhere. Jobs have dried up. Marriages have dried up. Homes have been taken when mortgages dried up. Alcohol and drugs dry up people's lives. Hurting people just dry up because no one seems to care. Hearts are the worst, though. They dry up because there's been nothing that refreshes. That bothers me. In fact, it scares me a little. Then I heard a man say, "The drier the grass, the quicker it burns when a fire ignites it." I thought about that. The drier the grass, the quicker it burns when a fire ignites it. It makes a lot of sense.

I began to pray, "Lord, the grass is dry. The stock market has gone crazy, gas prices are up, and jobs have become shaky. The dryness is everywhere. Now, Lord, begin to burn up the grass like a wildfire spreading over the land. Let the good news spread like a wind-driven storm. We need the fire now. Allow Your Spirit to ignite us. I'm asking for the fire first. The drier the grass, the more rapidly the fire spreads. We are dry. Send Your fire.

Aha Moments

"But then, Lord, I ask for a cooling, nourishing rain. I ask that after the fire has spread, You will send the rains to soak into the soil and the soul. And in each life that has been dried, allow the rain to water and cool and nourish. Then allow tender young sprouts to burst forth in their lives. Let all around them know that the dryness was needed to make the soil ready to receive the rain The result is freshness, just like the air smells after a springtime rain. Let there be a noticeable difference. After the dryness, spread the fire, then drench us with rain.

For Older Women Only

Lots of changes come with age—graying hair, receding hairlines, and hair that grows where it never has before. One of the advantages of growing older is that we've learned much and want to share it.

His name is Matt, and he's five years old. He's my grandson. I'm a much older female with all the aches, pains, and other attributes of age including a few hairs that appeared on my chin. I was desperately trying to make an impression (as adults often do) on this young man. I wanted to instill in him some of life's important lessons. They would be easier for me to teach him than for him to learn. I'd worked out a simple plan to impart wisdom, much as a mentor may tutor a young disciple. I prepared a few basic points packed solid with wisdom in easy words.

He was engrossed, looking straight into my face. Except for an occasional shutting and opening of the eyes, he was enraptured. Can you imagine my excitement? I knew I would remember this day, this moment, and this priceless portrait forever. As I paused to catch my breath and capture the wonder of the moment, he spoke. "Can I ask you a question?" I noticed he was gazing intently at my mouth and chin (trying to make sure he captured the answer to his question, I reasoned).

"Sure, please ask me anything you'd like."

Gazing at my chin, he asked, "Are you trying to grow a beard?"

Christmas Cards

While we may not be very good at either artwork or poetry, my husband and I composed and designed our Christmas cards. Each year, we took real pleasure in presenting personal cards to our friends and relatives. This one was written ten months after the diagnosis of cancer and after we experienced many of God's miracles during those months following the diagnosis—then came the holidays.

Remember Me

Upon his shoulders, his father hung
A coat of beauty, in colors flung.
It set him apart and made him proud
To wear that multicolored shroud.
Joseph called from darkened well;
Echoed voice against walls did swell.
"Brothers, please, how can this be?
Don't leave me here—remember me."

But soon the coat from shoulders shed
Was dipped in blood, darkening red.
The father clasped the coat and cried,

Grief-stricken, for his son had died.
Brought and sold to Ishmaelites;
Traveled desert day and night.
In Potiphar's house bound by stone,
Chained in spirit, desperately alone.
Once again, the cloak became
The object grabbed by Egyptian dame.
He left the garment, fled away;
Potiphar's wife would not have her way.
Into the dark prison cell he's flung.
What was to become of this slave undone?
Dreams unfolded to chef's decree:
"When you arrive, remember me."

Into the manger, we looked and gazed.
"Promised Messiah!" Voices raised.
"Messiah, yes—He's come at last.
Promise fulfilled, prophesized from past."
He grew and lived and walked among
Sinners, needy, salvation sung.
He healed and taught those who came;
He touched lips and limbs once lame.
He gathered on Passover's night.
Broke bread, poured wine by candlelight.
Then from His lips, love flowing free
In urgent whisper: "Remember Me.
As oft as cup and bread are given.
Remember Me, by agape driven.
Remember Me down through the ages.
Remember Me on life-written pages."

Then to a cross, He was led away—
Heaven's brightest and darkest day.
Heaven's glorious, most precious treasure,
Given for earth—no want, no measure.
With urgent need, we turn to view
The crosses holding thieves of two.
The one cried out in angry thrusts;
The other spoke from throat of dust.
"This man has done nothing wrong.
He is not man but heaven's song.
When You, Messiah, from earth are free—
When You're in heaven, remember me."
The tomb with stone sealed and tight
Opened to exhibit heaven's light.
But there, I hear it, can it be?
He asks again: "Remember Me."

Remember Me as you walk today.
Remember Me in all you say.
Remember Me; I gave My all.
Remember Me—on you I call.
And do you, child—now do you true?
Are you one of those chosen few,
Who remember Him and all He did?
He died for you in your lowly stead.

So what, dare I ask you, blunt and loud:
Do you remember Him? Are you proud,
Of His birth, His death, His blood poured out?
Do you His identity within you flout?

Aha Moments

> Remember Me. Remember Me.
> Wine, broken bread—look and see.
> Be one of those, the chosen few:
> For He, precious one, will remember you.

The previous twelve months were challenging. We experienced deep valleys and high mountaintops. The rod of God seemed ever present. I felt I would never stop the descent in the valleys, and then I began to experience that tender kiss of God. Then I began to soar, snatched from the valley of darkness, up and out, toward the sharp peaks of the mountains. I squinted my eyes in the radiance of sun-drenched, mountain-covering snow as clear and brilliant air tingled my face, and embraced the effervescence of all God had done for me. It took my breath away. Part of that experience was my God family. Those memories of my God family are precious. They are kinfolk, brothers and sisters who cried, laughed, and hurt with me; who made meals, called, and sent a ton of cards; who prayed and prayed. My God family provided the tender kiss of God, applied soothingly and with great compassion.

When you go through those tough waters, knowing that others are with you makes the journey bearable. When you see others walking a difficult path, your being there for them makes their pathways more walkable. That's what a God family is all about.

Message from a Thesaurus

I was preparing a presentation and needed a word. It was right on the tip of my tongue, but I couldn't recall what it was. It was a $25 word, but it fit perfectly what I needed to express—if I could just think of it. I went to the thesaurus on my computer. Regrettably, there is nowhere I can enter the definition of a word and have the computer provide the word for me. Maybe someone should develop a suruaseht (thesaurus spelled backward). I tried synonyms, but nothing came close. I was frustrated and tried for perhaps thirty minutes to locate the word. It was a critical part of the presentation, and I needed that exact $25 word to tie the whole thing together. I finally closed down the computer and completed my evening chores.

As I climbed into bed later that night, I still mentally scanned for that word, but nothing surfaced. Sleep came and went. I woke up around 3:00 a.m. and could not go back to sleep. I was restless, and on this rare occasion, I got up. Then I did something I never do. I went to our family room and cut on the TV at 3:15 a.m. *Frasier*, the sitcom from years ago, was on. The segment involved Frasier's son, Frederick, who was participating in a spelling contest. Just as I tuned in, the judges gave Frederick the word he was to spell. And there it was—the word I had searched for—given on a sitcom at 3:15 a.m. Not only given, but spelled correctly.

I realized that many years before that night, some comedy writers were preparing this skit. They needed a fairly difficult word—one that was a bit obscure—and one of them suggested my word. They put the word in the skit. Now, on a rerun years later, at 3:15 one morning, that years-old comedy routine would play. God showed me that His plan to provide that word for me had begun years ago. He woke me up in time to get to the TV at exactly the moment that the TV would warm up already tuned to the channel that would air the sitcom. It was His gift to me, prepared years ago and waiting for just the right moment to be presented. I turned the TV off and thanked my Father for His wonderful care in such a small matter. I went to the computer, found my notes, and entered the word. Content in my Father's care, I went back to bed and to sleep. Aha. What a caring God we have.

Are you still wondering what the word was? It was *hermeneutics*. How often would you expect to find that word in a sitcom? (It means "the study of the methodological principles of interpretation.")

Rivletts

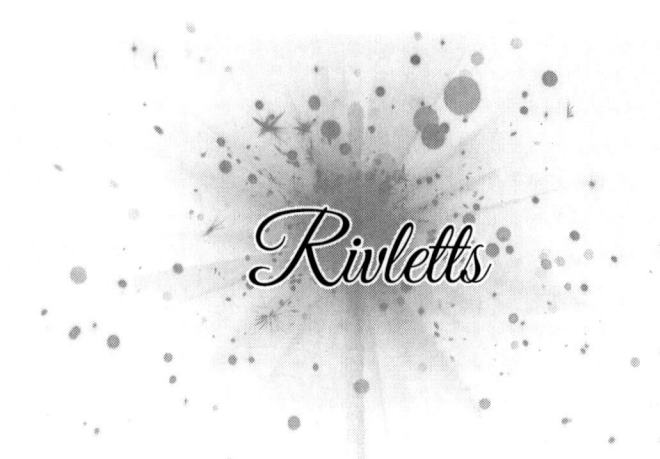

Don't look the word "rivletts" up in the dictionary. I don't think you'll find it, so let me explain what it means. Do you remember when you were a little kid and you waited for someone for what seemed like days? It was a gray day with cloudy skies and misty rain. Then your eye caught a look at the car window or windshield, and you'd see a burgeoning water droplet. It got bigger, and then ever so slowly, it began a downward race, gathering both moisture and speed. Perhaps it occasionally stopped, but eventually, like a windshield gully washer, it made its way to the bottom of the window. You would silently cheer on the victory, and as if drawn by an invisible magnet, your eye would spot another one.

Perhaps you got to experience a twin rivlett race where there were two growing water bubbles nearby, and the inevitable contest was on. You'd carefully watch both, betting on one, hoping it would be the first to start its cascade down the slope and win the race to the bottom. That's what rivletts are. Rivlett races helped pass many a waiting hour, although the sports broadcaster never announced the winners on the evening news.

Rivlett races crowd the memories of my childhood, and I find, even as an adult, that I engage in an occasional race from the enviable midfield box seat of my car (right behind the steering wheel) as I wait for someone or something. Misty rain, a windshield, and a need to wait allow me to once again experience rivlett races.

Not long ago, two of my friends asked me to pray about significant situations in their lives. These were beyond some of the more standard issues of not-too-serious illnesses, these were what I'd refer to as crossroad issues. With each friend, we presented these issues before the Lord. The first issue was resolved when one friend ran up to me and said, "You're not going to believe this. God has so wonderfully answered that critical issue. He not only answered it; He topped it off with icing on the cake." Then she began to recite how what seemed to be a disappointment and a major roadblock, was wonderfully revealed as a twist in the story with a surprise ending. Each and every detail had been woven to show God's wonderful answer to a three-week-long prayer request. We hugged, cried happy tears, rejoiced, and yelled a little. It was wonderful of our God to answer, and we thanked Him.

About two weeks later, pretty early in the morning, I had already had my cup of coffee, and the sun had begun its peek over the horizon. The phone rang. Early-morning calls can be scary, but this call came from the excited voice of the second friend. "I knew you'd be up. I couldn't send all of this in an e-mail, and I just had to tell you what has happened." She then relayed how the issue we'd prayed about was divinely answered. She also experienced icing on the cake. God not only answered the one prayer that was critical, but He also piled on a layer of icing above and beyond what was needed to what was wanted. And He gave not only what was wanted, but a double portion. As before, we praised, prayed, and praised again. Our God is good. I hung up the phone, still on a God high.

Then a rivlett caught my eye. It was just a small droplet. God had quickly (or so it seemed to me) answered their needs. I had prayed with them. God had heard. That was good. And I continued to rejoice in what they had received in answer. But what about me? The droplet got a little bigger. What about me? Again, the droplet grew. "God," I prayed as I breathed carefully, "Do you remember that issue I've been praying about for a long time? It sits there on Your desk in the inbox. It hasn't been answered. Their needs are no more urgent. Their requests came in *after* mine. You were quick to respond to them. What about me?"

The droplet gained momentum and started its cascade. More rapidly, the doubts began to gather. "What about me? Why not answer my request? Is it me? Is it that I don't have enough faith? Have I missed praying about this issue hard enough? What is wrong?" The rivlett race was on, and nothing could stop its path. It gathered momentum, finally crashing at the bottom of its course.

Then a still, small voice spoke patiently to my heart. "Child—oh, child. Have you forgotten all of the times I've answered your prayers? Your needs—I've taken care of everything. And just as I did for them, I will answer this current issue—but in the perfect time. Do you doubt Me? Do you doubt My love for you? Do you doubt that I have the ability to do whatever is needed? My answer for you will be perfect, just as My answer for them was perfect. But to be perfect, it must be at the perfect time. Wait and see what I will do, child. Grow your faith; that's part of the answer. You need a bit of growing time."

The rivlett race was over. My heart was humbled in sadness that I had ever doubted. I asked Him to forgive me for forgetting all He had done. I began a new rivlett race. This one was focused on the blessings I had received. I watched many cascading droplets run across the windshield of my mind. There, at His feet, I left the current issue for Him to answer in His time. (See Ecclesiastes 3:11.)

Brown and Gray

His name is Matt, and he's in kindergarten. He's my grandson and calls me "Bo." He thinks his teacher knows all there is to know (and she just may). Matt is a very practical guy. If you get to the door first, you are first in line. There is very little gray in his life. He has the answers. And he is not a frou-frou young man. You get the puzzle, find the pieces, finish it, and get on to the next task. When you're asked to draw a picture of your home, you draw the house. You don't draw people, dogs, trees, flowers, or curtains at the windows. You draw the house.

He is practical and to the point and does not believe in fluff. He hears the task assigned and gets the job done—period. And his answers are much that way. He doesn't embellish with a ton of words; he uses enough words to thoroughly get his point across, and that's it (unless you disagree with him). He's quick and efficient. He is usually the first to turn in his test or whatever assignment has been given.

On this particular day, his teacher gave the class an assignment. She said, "Most of you are five or six years old. I want you to use your imagination and draw a picture of how you will look in one hundred years." Tiny five-year-old fingers reached for crayons. As might be expected, many of the girls drew themselves wearing long, pink dresses. Others attempted a sitting portrait. The task went on, and like the smell of rubber burning at a raceway, the aroma that resulted from the smell of burning crayons spoke of intense concentration.

Matt was the first to finish. He wrote "Matt H." at the top of the paper, walked confidently to the front of the room, and placed his finished portrait on the teacher's desk. I should mention that art is not one of his top skills. His teacher thanked him and then looked questioningly at the portrait. It contained a brown oval placed horizontally on the paper next to a gray rectangle that was placed vertically. That was it—nothing more. Perhaps him with a gray beard, she thought, but that wasn't quite it. "Matt." She beckoned him back to the desk and asked, "I don't quite know what this is. Could you explain it to me please?"

"Sure," he said. "That is my grave, and that is my tombstone. In one hundred years, I will be dead." This was factual, and to him, it was not at all gruesome, just realistic. The teacher had to leave the room to laugh so hard she cried.

The Sapling

In our somewhat rural church, we have a group of men who love to hunt. On this particular day, two somewhat older guys, Jake and Will, who had been friends since grade school, started out in the crisp early morning dimness. Frost from the night before still crunched under their boots, and their breath seemed to crystalize in midair. Moving as quietly as possible, they sleuthed their way to an area where their luck had previously been good—and sure enough, a buck stood almost straight ahead.

In excited sign language, they motioned to each other that Will would move to the right and Jake to the left to get a better shot. Like actors in slow motion, they bent over, moving through the low shrubbery. They didn't want to alert the buck, and they didn't want to miss. Jake lost sight of the deer as he crouch-walked his way through the underbrush. Then, just off to his right, he heard the animal coming straight at him. He raised his gun, aimed at the movement, and fired.

Stop. Let's freeze the action here. The ammunition was fired; nothing could stop it. Look past the bullet. Focus on the target, just as Jake did after he'd fired. He realized that Will had made the bushes move. Will became the unintentional target. And Jake was a marksman; he rarely missed. I wish I could tell you that this was just a movie and that we could pause everything to stop and redo the scene. But we can't. In real life, we can't stop the action for a re-take.

Let's go back fifteen years and visit that same spot. The trees aren't quite as large as they are now, but everything else is pretty much the same. Fifteen years ago, there was a large oak tree, and it was a heavy acorn year. They seemed to fall by the tons. Squirrels dug holes and buried them deep or had a wonderful forest buffet lunch. On one particular day fifteen years ago, a squirrel picked up an acorn and was about to have lunch when a voice seemed to whisper, "Nay, don't eat that one; it's a bit scrawny. There's a much fatter one just over there." And sure enough, the squirrel looked a few feet away to a plump, golden acorn. Dropping the first acorn, he dashed to the other and devoured it. It was juicier and sweeter than any he had ever had. The first acorn rolled under a leaf, and as acorns have a habit of doing, it found itself buried on the forest floor.

When spring came, that acorn put down roots, and a small sprout popped from the forest moss into the warmth of springtime. Just about then, a rabbit happened by. As it eyed the tender sprout, a voice seemed to suggest, "There's a spot of tender, wild cabbage growing just a little further. I know you'd like that better." And sure enough, the rabbit hopped just a few more feet and had a delightful, satisfying breakfast of wild cabbage.

Move ahead a few years, and you'll see that the acorn has emerged into something almost three feet high, just right for the young doe that grazed in the area. There it was again—what seemed like a whisper: "No, my dear, you'd much rather munch on the moss that is growing just over there—lots of nutrients and on so much easier to digest." And she grazed on the moss, leaving the small tree to grow.

The years passed. The acorn grew as the summer sun made its way past the giants in the forest, allowing enough sunlight for the tree. For fifteen years, it grew. Oaks don't grow rapidly, and in those fifteen years, it became a nice sapling. Let's unfreeze the scene now. At bullet speed, Jake realized the outcome would be tragic. He didn't even breathe. He knew what would happen. The newspapers carried headlines like this every year, "man killed in hunting accident." The blood drained from his face.

Then he heard an awful drawing in of breath and a muted scream. He saw Will collapse into a heap. The deer, startled, fled. Jake rushed to Will, pushing past the thistles, briars, and undergrowth. As he reached Will, Jake leaned over, grabbing at Will's shoulders, expecting blood. None appeared initially. He tore open Will's jacket—nothing. Moments passed, but it seemed much longer. Will grabbed his leg. Jake rolled Will over and looked. And then he saw it—splinters embedded in the leg. There was no bullet—nothing more than a scratch. Only then did Jake realize that the bullet topped the sapling that stood just feet away. Once deflected, the bullet fell harmlessly to the ground. He felt relieved, thankful, and grateful. Jake began to breathe again, and color returned to his face. Jake helped Will to his feet, as the leg did hurt. They gratefully headed back to the car and a cup of hot coffee. Hunting was finished for the day.

God placed that acorn there many years before. God knew it would be needed, and He made sure that no rabbit, squirrel, or young doe nibbled on it. The sapling was in just the right spot for the moment it would be needed. God had a purpose for that tree. In your life right now, there are saplings that have grown. Some are grass-high and will not be needed for many more years, but there is one that will be needed soon. God has His eye on you and will provide a sapling. There's a forest full of them. Aha. They're just waiting patiently to be used when needed.

It Is Finished

When Jesus was on the cross, He cried out in agony, "It is finished." This is a strange statement to herald the beginning. When Jesus cried out, "It is finished," He opened heaven's gates to us. The beginning of eternal life was offered. What has the sound of the end was actually the joyous invitation to the beginning. From the cross, the words "it is finished" echoed through the pages of the Old Testament into the ears of Moses and Abraham, Isaac, Jacob, and Joseph. It caressed the childish ears of young Samuel and played on the harp strings of David. "It is finished" was the fulfillment of the prophecy and the beginning of the promise. Listen as those words ring out again in Revelation. When the seventh vial, the last bowl of judgment, is poured out, from the hallowed halls of heaven, those words echo again: "It is finished."

As it began, so now *ends* the promise. "It is finished" is no longer a joyous invitation but a crushing closure. God's time of open arms becomes His time of a closed fist, and that fist pounds down in saddened finality, proclaiming the end of the offering and the beginning of divine justice. So it is in our hearts. The invitation is there from the words of the cross: "It is finished." A nail-scarred hand reaches out to you. If we reject Him again, the mighty God will one day utter those words from which there is no reprieve: "It is finished."

Aha Moments

The hand of God can be open and inviting or closed in judgment. This is an awesome thought. God is an awesome God. Have you met my God? He is loving, kind and understanding. It is very simple—too simple for some. God wants you in His heaven. He's already paid the price of admission. You only need to call out to Him, knowing there is nothing else you can do, and you offer all of yourself to Him. There is no magic in the words themselves; the change comes when the heart speaks them. Say them with me now if you are truly ready to turn over your all for His all.

> God, I am a sinner. I have done nothing to deserve heaven. I repent. I turn away from all the wrong things I have done and turn to You to give me the ability to do right. I believe that Jesus Christ is the Son of God, was virgin-born, and lived, died, and rose again. His death—His life's blood—bought my way into heaven. I believe He spoke my name with His dying breath. And then Jesus rose again in order to conquer death for me. I give my life to You to live as You want me to. I'll mess up, I'm sure, but I trust you to forgive that, too. Today, I become a child of God. In Jesus' name, amen.

Do you feel different? I hope so. So what's next? First, find a good place of worship, to learn more about Him. Then you will begin to walk the path in resurrection power.

Surprise!

I like surprises. That's what I like about Easter celebrations: I like finding the hidden eggs. Once they're found, there's a surprise inside. The story of Jesus is like that too.

The birth of Jesus was a surprise—even to His mother. She was told by an angel that Jesus was going to be born. And then she received another surprise as an angel appeared in a dream to His earthly father. The shepherds were totally surprised by angels that suddenly appeared on a dark night. And then the shepherds (like those hidden Easter eggs) had to look for Him and found Jesus in a manger that was hidden behind the houses and inns.

Did you already think about the wise men? They were surprised to see a new star in the sky. They followed that star to find the hidden surprise of a newborn king living in the small town of Bethlehem. There were puzzles and surprises throughout His life. Jesus told parables that puzzled His disciples and other people who listened to them. So Jesus explained what they meant.

There were surprises in His life. He feed five thousand people, healed the sick, raised Lazarus from the dead, and walked on water. (I wonder if His feet got wet.) He was full of surprises, and I think He smiled a lot when He saw the look on people's faces.

He loved even the people who weren't easy to love, like the people with bad sores or leprosy and the man who lived in a cemetery. And when grownups tried to keep the children away, He said, "I love them; let them come to me." He loved all the way to the cross. And He kept on loving even when the soldiers hurt and screamed at Him. Jesus said, "Forgive them, Father, for they don't know what they are doing." He loved all the way to the tomb.

When they placed His body in the tomb and rolled the stone in place, everybody thought it was over. They thought He was dead. But Jesus wasn't just a person who had lived a good life; He was the Son of God. Surprise! Jesus conquered death. Did you ever wonder why the stone was rolled away? It was not so He could get out but so that we could see in. The best surprise of all is not an empty tomb but a living Savior.

Porpoise Syndrome

My work in a company that had a worldwide reputation of excellence provided many wonderful opportunities to observe just how people interacted with each other. One of the unique opportunities was hiring second career people. These were individuals who had retired from their primary positions but wanted some activity to get them out of the house. The saying, "When a man retires, a wife gets twice the husband with only half the salary," often reflected reality. This observation is based on the men who had retired from executive positions only to find that they missed the camaraderie of the workplace. The jobs they did for us were a bit menial and required physical activity both inside the work facility as well as outside. As an additional benefit, these retired individuals brought with them the work ethics of yesteryear, imparting those high standards to a younger generation.

I have never studied marine biology, but I am told that there is a phenomenon that is played out time and again with porpoises. Since porpoises are mammals and must rise to the surface to breathe, it is essential that this continue at all times. When giving birth, the female porpoise will often lose her concentration as the contractions occur and she will sink below the surface. Other porpoises will gather near her, nudge her firmly with their noses, and bump her back to the surface. This occurs time and again; those around her watch, move in, and with a firm bump, propel her back to the surface for life-giving breath.

As these retired men came to work, camaraderie was formed at the various company sites. And then one of the men would lose his wife. He would take a leave of absence to attend to all the necessary details but not return to work. His coworkers would begin to call him, checking to see just how he was doing. They gave gentle bumps. One after the other, they called. And then the bumps became more firm and not quite so gentle. More force was needed to get him to the surface. They made comments such as, "Hey, man, I'm having to work extra hard to carry your part of the work. Come on back, now." *Bump.* "What's with you? You're slacking off too long. Get it back in gear." *Bump.* "Bad example you're sitting for these young guys. Pull it together." This was a hard bump, but it was needed. "Man, get back here or I'll get your…" That was a really hard bump.

Soon, we'd see him back at work. Slaps on the back were given (more bumps), and as he was surrounded by his friends and the pain of his loss lessened. The men worked shoulder to shoulder, and the porpoise syndrome proved a life-saving technique to allow the one who was sinking beneath the surface to breathe again. A sad chapter had closed, but with his friends, he would be ready to begin a new chapter and help bump someone when the situation presented itself.

Poinsettias

We all have times in our lives when there are issues to be faced—tough times that must be walked through, as there is simply no way to walk around them. I found myself in such a place. It began in November. The issue entered my life like a tsunami—overwhelming, unexpected, rising slowing and then plowing through with merciless accuracy, undermining much that I held sacred and dear. I had worked hard to keep home and job separate and continued that same path. Home was where the problem was.

Since home was no longer the oasis it had been, I retreated to the security and protection of my job. I had a position I loved dearly and had recently acquired a new (and untested) boss. My office was on the corner, where the CEO passed when entering and exiting the building. He was a great CEO whose business savvy was tempered with compassion. I was always an early-to-work person and relished those times in the office before the hustle and bustle of the day began. To cope with this current issue, I began arriving even earlier. I could focus my thoughts on the tasks at hand and force the issues of home to the far recesses of my mind—at least for a while.

Often the CEO and I walked in together, exchanged a few pleasantries, and then each continued on our way to complete our to do list. Working throughout the day, solving problems, and occupying myself with the demands of business provided a wonderful respite from what had to be faced all too soon. The CEO would stick his head around the office door and say goodnight. Except for the janitorial team, I was the last one in the building. This same pattern continued for weeks. I simply did not want to leave the security of my office to face issues that presented themselves at home. And so I worked long hours, safe and secure in my office cave. I received accolades for the results of those long hours, and that praise was like a soothing ointment to my soul.

The holidays were coming, but there was nothing in my heart that reverberated with the celebration of what had previously been a loved season. One night, the CEO was leaving and stopped by to say goodnight. He left, and I returned to the task at hand. Moments later, he reappeared. "Mind if we chat for a minute?" he asked.

"Absolutely fine," I answered, and I adapted a professional, everything-is-right-with-the-world tone.

"I've noticed the amount of work coming out of your office, and it is excellent. But I'm concerned. Are you having to put in these long hours because the new guy isn't doing all that he should be?"

I assured him that the new man on board was not the reason. I was just anxious to see that everything was completed before the end of the year. He seemed reassured and left. I was relieved. My performance had kept my secret well hidden, and my endeavor to keep home and job separate was secure.

Moments later, the CEO returned. "Hi," he began. "I'm still concerned. You seem to be here from sunup to sundown and beyond. I feel that there is something I need to know about the level of work required of you."

I assured him again that this was just a work ethic issue for me. I enjoyed seeing projects completed and presented as they should be.

This time, he moved closer to the desk and seated himself on the edge. "I'm asking you to honestly share with me what is making all of this necessary," he stated.

The intensity of his look and the honesty of his inquiry caused the wall I had so carefully put up to crumble. I explained that there was a personal issue and that working helped me avoid all that must be dealt with. Work was my retreat, and I had been putting in long hours to avoid facing issues outside of work. I explained that I had made a commitment to keep work and home separate and had not shared the issue with anyone.

He was gracious and apologized many times for intruding. He thanked me for being honest, assured me of his confidence, and apologized once more for pushing the issue. Then he left. I returned to the task at hand, feeling a bit better that finally someone else knew—someone I could trust.

The holidays quickly approached. It was Christmas Eve, and I did not want to go home. The house would be empty, cold, and vacant. Someone needed to stay late at the office, and I volunteered, finally leaving when there was no other option. The twinkling lights of the season and anxious driving of others made my journey more difficult. I had nothing to look forward to when I arrived home. A cold, penetrating rain mirrored the emotions of my soul.

I arrived home and unlocked the door. Sitting in the middle of my living room was the biggest poinsettia I had ever seen. (I would learn later that a neighbor with whom I had entrusted a key allowed entrance to the floral delivery person.) I walked over to the beautiful plant, found the card, and read a warmly written note. "I understand, I know you are alone, I know it is tough, you are valued as a person and as a friend, I am here for you…" and on and on. That lovely handwritten note and the giant poinsettia plant were from the CEO. Despite his enormously hectic schedule, the demands of both business and family, he had taken time to care about one person in his very large corporation. He cared. He took time. He called a florist, wrote a note, and shared of himself.

My holiday was brightened. Since that time, I have been offered positions with other companies with better benefits and higher salaries, but not one of those companies could offer me what was provided by that gift—a sense of worth and caring. For the price of poinsettias, that CEO and his company provided something no other group could come close to matching. The price of poinsettias evidenced the worth of a person. The investment of time and care made a huge difference, warmed my heart, and made the holidays what they were meant to be – a season of caring.

Now I Lay Me Down to Sleep

Stop for a moment and think about someone who is close to your heart. I mean it. Put down the book, and think about that person. What are his or her likes, dislikes, concerns, and anxieties? Why do you love this person? How did you find out all of those things? How did you get to know him or her? Did you build a relationship?

The answer is the same with prayer. You build that relationship by spending time, talking, and listening. Do you do all the talking? Does the other person? Communication means getting and giving information. So how do we gain intimacy with God?

Text messages and quick e-mails allow us to share with others those events that are happening. It is like that with God too. I call these popcorn praises. An immediate 'pop', much like popcorn in a microwave. It is just one kernel at a time. Pop. That tiny kernel explodes. Throughout the day as something of beauty is displayed, a pop-up of praise, directed to our Father, is a good thing. We see a bluebird. The sunrise is especially beautiful. Or we find a parking place really close to the store when we are in a major hurry. Popcorn praise helps me thank the Giver.

Aha Moments

Arrows are sent individually and their aim is for a specific target. Arrow prayers are much like that. I use them for urgent needs and for a specific issue. As I drive, I may see that a pretty serious accident has occurred. I send up an arrow prayer: "Lord, please be with those people who are hurt and frightened, and please Lord, if they have never confronted their mortality and their eternity, please let them have a chance to do so." Perhaps I pray an arrow prayer when I get a call from a loved one announcing a medical diagnosis that could be serious. I will pray longer and deeper later, but at the moment, it is an arrow prayer sent directly to the throne of God, asking for His help, calm, and peace on all involved.

Popcorn praise and arrow prayers are good. But I need a real conversation, an ongoing conversation that reveals more of the Father to me and more of me to the Father. I know God knows all, and He knows more about me than I do. But it is important for me to reveal myself to Him. This helps me be real, and I don't have to pretend to be so great when I reveal all of myself and acknowledge just what I am. I schedule a time to meet with Him and, for me, the best time is early in the morning. No one is around, and the day is fresh and unspoiled. I'm no super saint, so if I don't get it done first thing, I will allow other things to interfere, or at best, I'll squeeze God in somewhere. In our day of mobility, I like to begin with a landline connection—a defined time and place where I am less likely to be disturbed.

As I keep this daily appointment, I mentally picture a lake. There is a well-worn but not overly used pathway and a big boulder near the lake. Next to that large boulder is a much smaller one. I can see the trees and moss along the path and feel the gentle warm breeze as it comes off the lake, and in that very private meeting place, I meet with Him.

He sits on the larger boulder, and no matter what time I get there, He's waiting patiently and expectantly. I position myself on the small rock and look up into His kind, gentle face. He is focused on me, and love flows out from Him to me. I reach up carefully and grasp the hem of his tunic, much like the woman who touched the hem of His garment(Luke 8:43-44). I love sitting at His feet. Sometimes I just sit there, relishing the privilege of being close to Him. Because He knows me so well, our conversation goes beyond words.

ACTS, STAC, TACS, CATS, SCAT, and CAST are acronyms that help me pray.
    C—confession
    A—adoration
    S—supplication
    T—thanks

My personal prayer time works best for me if I CAST. I confess to get any sin or disruption in my relationship with God out of the way, enabling clear communication. The tabernacle mentioned in the Old Testament was set up so people went to the altar to sacrifice first. And I follow a similar process. I offer the sacrifice of confession first. In the courtyard just before entering the tabernacle, the 'stuff' of life was left, burned on the altar, allowing entrance inside the tabernacle. Consider all that was on the outside, the heat of the desert, dryness of the air, smell of animals, and noise. It is as if God could not be heard amid the distractions of life. Leaving all of life's confusions outside at the altar, I am ready to move inside to begin to worship.

Inside the tabernacle of prayer, the smells and noise are barely recognized. The heat and oppression of the day have gone and the shelter of the tent provides a cool oasis. No requests or confessions; just worship Him for who He is, the holy, sovereign Lord. I marvel at His perfection, mercy, fathomless grace, boundless love, creativity, patience, and majesty. God is the sustainer of all. I worship Him. I picture myself before that altar of incense, simply praising, worshipping, and adoring Him for those attributes that allow me to come near to Him. I strive to allow worship to be a large portion of my time with Him.

In this time of adoration, I simply want to adore the Maker. Consider that the Sovereign God is *all* that He is. Adore the giver, not just the gift. To keep my prayer life fresh, I try to express my love for Him in different ways. Dance before Him; I suggest something slow and swirly, as it's less risky. Sing Him a song you've written just for Him, compose poetry, raise your hands in praise, twirl, do an arm dance, or make finger fireworks. (Close all your fingers together like a rosebud and then explode them outward and upward.) Write a letter to Him if you're a person who journals. Lay prostrate, draw Him a picture—take a risk. He'll love it and love you for wanting to do something special for Him. I've paraphrased Exodus 15:1–21. At times, I read this out loud to the Lord, and you may find it meaningful as well. Try something different, and only worship.

Next, I move to supplication. This is when I ask God to touch people's lives. I present the problems, challenges, and issues with which I or others need God's help. Do you know how many names God has in the Bible? I can't answer that, but I do know that He is called the God of peace, the God who heals, and many more. I compiled a list of names, and when I approach a particularly tough issue, I use one of those many names of God that fits that situation.

I notice that I ask God for a lot of things. More and more, I'm convinced that I should not be in prayer for the physical part of life as much as for the spiritual. I certainly pray for people to be healed, minds to be calmed, and relationships to be repaired, but I have learned that sometimes those tough times are spiritual growth times. My prayers now seem to focus more on asking the Lord to walk with the person *through* the tough time rather than to remove the tough issues.

That brings me to the last part of my prayer time—thanksgiving. I like to think this is the dessert part of the prayer. The appetizer may be good, the soup and salad tasty, and the main course filling, but you usually remember the dessert. I want to leave a good taste when I'm finished, so I end my talk-time with God with thanksgiving. I tell Him what I appreciate that He has given me—the little things (like sprinkles on top of a cupcake) and the big things. I try to notice exactly what He gives me each day. Gifts may be as simple as not letting me hit the squirrel that played dart-and-run as I traveled or something as major as hearing that a friend's diagnosis was benign. I thank Him for the colossal things like salvation, His suffering, His cross, or His patience with me too. Prayer is packed full as I CAST it all on Him. Then I wait, listening for His voice knowing He will speak to me.

And the Rest of the Story

My husband and I are dog rescuers—at least, I am. I'm a sucker for trusting eyes that seem to say, *I don't know what I did wrong, but if you take me home, I promise I won't do it again.* Nothing can upset me more than to see someone hurt an animal, place the creature on a chain and ignore it, or to put a dog in a crate where it has no room to move and leave it there for hours. When we decided to adopt a new member to our family, our trips included visits to wonderful facilities that are dedicated to rescuing canines and felines who have been neglected and abused. That's how we were introduced to a delightful new family member.

There was an immediate bond when we were introduced to a Great Pyrenees. He had been crate-confined for many hours each day and was punished when his bladder could no longer hold it. There had been little affection or social interaction with people or other dogs, and he had rarely been groomed. This bedraggled beauty entered our home. A bath, brushing, and a few good meals revealed that he was a gorgeous creature with a flowing coat of which he was quite proud. A large, fenced yard and the run of the house made him confident that he was, in fact, home. He was devoted to us.

The rescue group required that all adopted pets be neutered, and we complied.

In keeping with our love for him, we took him on top-open drives in our Suzuki. He sat in the backseat and allowed his mane to flow majestically in the wind. I imagined him saying, *Hey, all you girl dogs, eat your heart out. I'm quite the catch.*

I would tactfully remind him, "You can't do anything about any romantic encounters, you know."

To this, I imagined he would respond, *Yeah, but they don't know that.* And so we traveled many enjoyable miles together, all three of us smiling contently.

My husband was a car enthusiast who kept all of our vehicles clean and shining. He rarely allowed me to help with the washing and waxing process. I simply did not do it like he thought it should be done. Washing was a carefully orchestrated process with great attention to detail. He had several brushes, from scrubbing brushes to paintbrushes to toothbrushes, that were assigned to various washing processes. And he loved the Suzuki. We joked that it was a car with an attitude. Though little in size, it screamed big in attitude. Since we used it primarily for fun adventures on the weekend with our faithful companion, the car did seem to shout, "I'm having fun; just try and stop me."

A Saturday often involved an early morning drive to yard sales with our dog in the backseat, his platinum coat flowing wonderfully, the pungent fresh air intermingled with the aroma of hot coffee. My husband was smug in knowing I couldn't buy much, as the car would contain only small purchases. After our return, the car would undergo a thorough cleaning, including a special treatment to keep the vinyl top gleaming white. Garage-kept, the Suzuki would be parked safely inside for a trip the next week.

Aha Moments

We had many great experiences and lots of memory-making days. One Saturday afternoon, I noticed that my husband seemed out of sorts. A bit of wifely inquiry (I refuse to call it nagging) revealed that he had lost his wedding ring. He never took it off, and it had seemed to be secure on his finger. Much time was devoted to our search, but we did not have a clue as to where it was or how it had been lost. Even though the search continued for weeks, we were unable to find the ring. After a few months, I purchased a replacement and the matter was closed. We continued those wonderful Saturday adventures, and the car accumulated many miles and memories. The ride was far from smooth, but we enjoyed the rough ride that only those who have ridden in (and enjoyed) this type of transportation will understand. And the car continued to receive a thorough cleaning each week before being nestled back into its place.

Years went by. Regrettably, our faithful dog was eventually diagnosed with cancer, and we had to tearfully say good-bye. My husband and I continued to enjoy Saturday outings, although they were not quite the same without our backseat companion. And then my husband died. After some months, I decided the Suzuki would only rust away as I had no need for it any more. This conclusion was reached when our mechanic said, "You'll have to get new tires; these are dry-rotting." I'm not much of a believer in coincidences. (God-incidences are another thing.) But a good friend of my husband approached me and asked if I would be willing to sell the Suzuki; his son wanted it. We agreed, and the deed was done. I felt good placing our aging but well-kept vehicle in the care of someone I knew would continue to keep it in good shape.

A few weeks after the sale, the friend approached me one morning just before church. He said he needed to talk to me. His eyes welled with tears. I was concerned, as I could tell this could be hard to hear. We found a bench in the church hallway and sat down. He began talking about the Suzuki, and I was concerned that he had found some significant problem with the car. I made an immediate decision to return the purchase price and take it back. His story continued as I listened intently. He had been washing the Suzuki, and as he cleaned the backside of the front bumper, he hit something. He looked closely and found a wedding ring sitting there. He handed it to me. Was this, he asked, my husband's? Yes, it was.

We both cried. We could only assume that due to a soapy hand, the ring had slipped off and fallen behind the bumper. Why hadn't it bounced off during all the bumpy miles? Why in any washing since hadn't my husband discovered it? But there it sat, calmly waiting to be found. We sat there and cried, prayed, and thanked God for sending a gentle reminder that we are never out of His sight or care. Memories flooded back through those tears. The ring, now safely in my jewelry box, reminds me frequently how much our Lord knows, cares, and enjoys surprising us with His precious love.

Epilogue

The stories and whispers of God still continue. There have been lots of events after those you've just read. The company for which I worked for thirty years was sold. I was left without a job and wasn't yet eligible for Social Security. But God provided. He continues to provide events that shape and change my life in wonderful ways. The part I like best is that He continues to whisper secret messages meant just for me as He gathers me close to His heart. "Child, did you get the message I just sent?" He has messages for you too. Draw close to His heart, and listen. He's waiting to hear you say, "Aha, I got it."

CPSIA information can be obtained at www.ICGtesting.com
Printed in the USA
BVOW07s1251091114

374199BV00001B/2/P

9 781462 410026